GRANTSMANSHIP
for Small Libraries
and
School Library Media Centers

GRANTSMANSHIP
for Small Libraries
and
School Library Media Centers

Sylvia D. Hall-Ellis
Doris Meyer
Frank W. Hoffmann
Ann Jerabek

Edited by Frank W. Hoffmann

1999
Libraries Unlimited, Inc.
Englewood, Colorado

LIBRARIES UNLIMITED, INC.
P.O. Box 6633
Englewood, CO 80155-6633
1-800-237-6124
www.lu.com

Library of Congress Cataloging-in-Publication Data

Grantsmanship for small libraries and school library media centers /
    Sylvia D. Hall-Ellis ... [et al.] ; edited by Frank W. Hoffmann.
        xiii, 173 p. 19x26 cm.
        Includes bibliographical references and index.
        ISBN 1-56308-484-8
        1. Library fund raising--United States. 2. Proposal writing for
    grants--United States. 3. Small libraries--United States--Finance.
    4. School library finance--United States. 5. Instructional
    materials centers--United States--Finance. I. Hall-Ellis, Sylvia
    D.   II. Hoffmann, Frank W., 1949-
    Z683.2.U6G73   1999
    025.1'1—dc21   98-31247
                                                              CIP

Contents

INTRODUCTION ix

1—PLANNING: The Core of Grant Development 1
- A. Planning Defined 2
- B. The Rationale for Planning 4
- C. Readiness for Planning 4
  1. Historical Commitment to Planning 5
  2. The Reward System for Staff Contributions 5
  3. Culture, Size, and Complexity of the Organization 6
  4. Rate of Growth 6
  5. Financial Resources 6
  6. Access and Availability of Information . . . 7
  7. Willingness to Take Risks 7
- D. General Guidelines for the Pre-Development Planning Process 9
- E. Calendar Development 10
- F. Planning Meetings 15
  1. Initial Planning Meeting 15
  2. Conceptual Design Meeting 17
- G. Decisions Relating to Proposal Preparation . . 18
  1. Writing and Editing Issues 18
  2. Document Formatting Issues 19

2—PROJECT DESIGN 25
- A. The Importance of a Lucid Mission Statement 26
- B. Project Goal Development 26
  1. Goal Development in Public School Districts 28
  2. Goal Development in Public Libraries . . 29

2—PROJECT DESIGN (*continued*)

    C. The Relationship Between the Project Goal Statement
               and Project Objectives 30
    D. Conceptual Design of the Project 33
        1. Preliminary Checklists 33
        2. Methodologies 35
    E. The Dynamic Process Underlying Project Design 37
        1. Laying the Foundation for a Collaborative Effort 37
        2. Program of Action in Preparing the Team
            for Project Design 37
    F. Project Management 41
        1. Establishment of a Project Advisory Group 41
        2. Training for Advisory Group Members 42
        3. Project Management in Public School Districts 42
        4. Project Management in Public Libraries 43
    G. Parental Involvement with the Project 44

3—PROJECT NARRATIVE 45

    A. Proposal Functions 48
    B. Components of the Proposal 49
        1. Cover Sheet 49
        2. Abstract 50
        3. Table of Contents 50
        4. Introduction 50
        5. Needs Statement 51
        6. Goals and Objectives 52
        7. Project Design 53
        8. Budget 55
        9. Evaluation Design and Research Implications 55
      10. Dissemination of Findings, Results, Products 57
      11. Plan for Future Spending 58
      12. Appendices 59
    C. Cover Letter 60
    D. Proposal Writing, Design, and Organization Guidelines 60

4—PROJECT PERSONNEL 65

    A. Project Staffing Requirements 65
    B. Local Personnel Available to the Project 66
    C. Functional Capabilities Statements for Key Project Personnel . . . 66
        1. Project Director 66
        2. Other Personnel 68
        3. Library Media Specialist 69
    D. Provisions and Assurances 69
        1. Hiring and Employment Compliances 69
        2. Government Compliances 70

5—BUDGET DEVELOPMENT 71

A. The Role of the Budget. 71
B. Types of Budgets 71
C. Budget Preparation 72
D. Additional Budgeting Considerations 77
   1. The Influence of Funding Agencies on Budget Formatting . . 77
   2. Matching Funds and In-Kind Contributions 77
   3. Budget Adjustments and Amendments. 78
   4. Contract Negotiations 78
   5. Subcontracts. 79

6—PROJECT EVALUATION 81

A. Overview of the Evaluation Process 81
B. Evaluation Methods 82
   1. Formative Evaluation 82
   2. Summative Evaluation 83
C. Data Collection Methods. 83
   1. Quantitative Data Collection 84
   2. Qualitative Data Collection. 84
D. Evaluation Teams 84
   1. Internal Evaluation Teams 85
   2. External Evaluation Teams. 85

7—AFTER THE PROPOSAL 87

A. Constructive Activities for the Interim Period Prior
   to the Notification of Grant Award (NOGA) 87
B. Strategies for Successful Grant Recipients. 89
   1. Actions Immediately Following the Notification
     of Grant Award 89
   2. Guidelines for the Negotiation Process Between
     the Funder and Grant Recipient 89
   3. Project Implementation. 90
C. Strategies for Organizations Failing to Obtain Grant Funding . . . 94
   Poor Grantsmanship Practices. 95
   Resubmitting the Proposal and Seeking Other Funding Sources. . 98

   APPENDICES
     A—ANNOTATED BIBLIOGRAPHY 101
     B—FREQUENTLY ASKED QUESTIONS
       ABOUT GRANTSMANSHIP 115
     C—GLOSSARY. 127

   INDEX 157

Introduction

Few educators or librarians have been able to carry out their professional responsibilities without being introduced to the grantseeking process. Their interest may have started with a slowly building curiosity that was further fed by attendance at conferences or site-based workshops. On the other hand, it could have begun as a tentative involvement stimulated by the desire of administrators to mine this mother lode of funding possibilities.

While the larger libraries have generally been the most involved grantseekers in the past, the current financial picture—i.e., a leveling off of local, tax-based support, an increasing number of corporate and private donors available to fund worthy projects—combined with new educational challenges related to areas such as distance learning, the role of technology in the dissemination of information, etc., has made it imperative that smaller institutions, most notably public libraries and school media centers, also become actively committed to the process. However, small libraries are frequently unprepared to make a smooth transition into grantsmanship, lacking both the resources and staff expertise to effectively compete with their larger colleagues. Recognizing that any grantseeker must go after funding one step at a time, *Grantsmanship for Small Libraries and School Library Media Centers* focuses on the fundamentals of the process. Presuming little or no background knowledge on the part of the reader, the book will guide one through the primary stages comprising the grant development process:

1. Planning
2. Project Design
3. Project Narrative
4. Project Personnel
5. Budget Development
6. Project Evaluation
7. Supplementary Materials

One of the more confusing aspects of the grantseeking process has to be differentiating between the diverse array of grants. One source has noted 19 types along with examples of each:

Challenge Grant: money used as a magnet to attract additional funds. The Memorial Public Library receives $100,000 as a challenge grant to expand its collection.

Conference Grant: money to cover the expenses of holding a conference or seminar. The Keystone Center for Continuing Education receives $5,000 to support its Keystone Workshop Series.

Construction Grant: money for building construction. The Blue Lake Fine Arts Camp receives $65,000 for construction of a rehearsal hall.

Consulting Grant: money to hire consultants for an organization or project. The Unity Church receives $50,000 to hire a financial consultant to develop a long-term financial plan.

Demonstration Grant: money to demonstrate or prove that a particular project or idea actually works. The National Council on the Aging receives $70,000 for a demonstration program in student-provided services for the elderly.

Dissemination Grant: money to spread the results or funding of a successful project. The Project on Helping receives $23,000 to examine various aspects of volunteerism and to disseminate findings to local nonprofit organizations.

Endowment Grant: money to be kept permanently and invested to provide continued income to an organization. Harvard University receives $90,000 to support a permanent endowment for the Center for Hellenic Studies; the income will be used toward stipends for Junior Fellows and library and publication costs.

Equipment Grant: money to purchase new or replacement equipment. The Fellowship of Christian Athletes receives $75,000 toward the purchase and installation of computer equipment.

General Purpose Grant: money to further the general purpose or work of an organization rather than for a specific purpose. The Chicago Theatre Group receives $30,000 for general purpose support of the Goodman Theatre.

Land Acquisition Grant: money to purchase real estate property. Beloit College receives $75,000 toward the purchase of land to expand campus parking facilities.

Matching Grant: money to match funds provided by another donor. The Texas Panhandle Heritage Foundation receives $50,000 for matching support toward operating reserve fund.

Operating Grant: money to cover the daily costs of running an existing program or organization. The Mount Sinai Medical Center receives $10,000 for operating support.

Planning Grant: money to assess the need for and develop plans to implement a project. Montgomery County receives $25,000 to assess the feasibility of developing a rural health care delivery system.

Publication Grant: money to publish a report, book, magazine, or other publication. The New York Public Library receives $200,000 to support the publication costs of a new catalog describing its fine arts collection.

Renovation Grant: money to renovate, remodel, or rehabilitate property. Babson College receives $300,000 for the renovation of the Sir Isaac Newton Library.

Research Grant: money to cover costs of investigations or clinical trials. The Salk Institute for Biological Studies receives $10,000 for biological and medical research.

Seed Grant: money to start up or establish a new product or organization. Marquette University receives $15,000 to develop pilot data on causes of hypothermia.

Special Project Grant: money to support specific projects or programs as opposed to general purpose grants. Planned Parenthood receives $20,000 to survey teen attitudes toward adoption counseling.

Training Grant: money to train or instruct others in a method, technique, or procedure. The American Red Cross receives $25,000 for training programs in life-saving techniques geared to volunteers.

An understanding of these grant types can assist in either describing or redefining a proposed project. This categorization process facilitates efforts at matching your organization's strengths with the priorities of potential funders. Such comparisons, in turn, lead to the identification of marketing strategies for the proposal.

Given the fact that funders generally choose to work with known commodities, organizations new to the grants arena are readily apt to become discouraged. In order to circumvent the "catch-22" situation of needing to establish a record as a successful grant getter before obtaining a grant, the following strategies should be considered:

1. Include individuals in the proposal who already have a significant degree of experience with your targeted sponsor. If you lack credibility with the sponsor, borrow credibility from those known to the sponsor by having them serve as project co-directors or consultants.

2. Apply to sponsors with which you or members of your organization have established contacts and relationships. Use existing networks to help establish credibility.

3. Concentrate funding efforts on sponsors that have a history of taking on the uninitiated and the inexperienced. Some sponsors pride themselves on funding "high-risk, high-return" projects and organizations. They are willing to fund the "organizational underdog." Your prospect research, particularly a review of prior funding history, will help reveal such sponsors.

4. Demonstrate any crossover experience you might have had with programs of similar magnitude and complexity. Often you can cite experience managing other projects or personnel that will help successfully administer your proposed project.

5. Provide independent certifications and endorsements of qualifications from known authorities. This represents another means of borrowing credibility; i.e., respected experts can testify to your integrity.

6. Invite sponsors for an on-site visit or offer to visit them to discuss and demonstrate capability. This will provide you a first-hand opportunity to show the crispness of your organizational management skills.

7. Begin by requesting nonfiscal support. Sponsors often provide grants for things other than money; e.g., technical assistance, equipment donations, executive loan programs. This gives you a "foot in the door" of your target sponsor. If the experience is a positive one for both parties, the likelihood of receiving subsequent fiscal support from the sponsor increases notably.

8. Piggyback on the coattails of another organization or consortium with successful grant experience. In other words, join forces with others to build your credibility in subsequent proposals.

Above all, the success of the proposal depends upon your ability to convince the funder that a decision to provide support will pay dividends for that organization. Regarding a corporation, these benefits might include:

1. An improved image.

2. Enhanced corporate environs, covering areas such as ecology, transportation, communication, etc.

3. An upgraded benefits package, relating to new or better health programs, cultural activities, recreational facilities, etc.

4. A better pathway to attaining organizational goals; e.g., the provision of previously unavailable resources, the implementation of more effective training techniques, the development of new services.

Inexperienced grantseekers are likely to find grantsmanship a confusing, sometimes intimidating, process. Every effort has been made to cover the full spectrum of grantsmanship in a lucid, straightforward manner. In short, this book is devoted to providing the information necessary for librarians and educators to become effective members of grant development teams. The insights included in its seven chapters and three appendices are based upon experiences of professional grantseekers whose occupational backgrounds encompass school districts, state-supported region service centers, public libraries, higher education, private consulting, and entrepreneurial information services. The book's authors reiterate that ultimate success in grantsmanship, however, comes only with practice-based effort, combined with the commitment to turning temporary setbacks (i.e., proposal rejections) into eventual grant awards.

1

Planning

The Core of Grant Development

The writing of a successful grant proposal—one that ultimately secures funding—requires a well-designed plan. The planning process is a collaborative effort built around the individual and group contributions of a grant development team. Group members must share responsibilities for proposal development activities as well as a commitment to secure funding. Within an educational setting, an effective team should include administrators (principals, assistant principals, appropriate department heads), classroom teachers (the experts regarding instructional strategies in the educational environment), librarians (frequently considered to be active participants in the teaching program), curriculum specialists (program directors), support staff, faculty members from academic institutions, business and industry leaders, technology specialists, consultants, internal and external evaluators, a coordinator of grants development and management, students, and parents.

Self-directed professional teams are the key to effective grantsmanship. Tasks that team members can perform include researching funding sources (particularly federal and state governments, and agencies within the private sector), analyzing requests for proposals (RFPs) and requests for applications (RFAs) from funding sources, conducting local needs assessments, surveying the available literature to identify research-based models and "best practices" sites (see "Visits to 'Best Practices' Sites" in Chapter 2), inviting collaborators to participate in the project, and writing components of the proposal.

A. Planning Defined

The teamwork approach begins with a mutual commitment to planning. Planning is, in essence, a stratagem for doing, arranging, or producing something. In a library setting (or broader educational environment) planning will usually result in providing a service for, or imparting knowledge and skills to, a specific target group. Regarding proposal development, planning is ongoing in nature, spanning the entire grantseeking process. Step by step, this process includes

1. developing a conceptual design for the project and budget;

2. securing organizational approval to submit the grant proposal;

3. researching and identifying potential funding sources;

4. requesting guidelines and application forms;

5. writing the grant proposal;

6. submitting the proposal to the funding source on or before the deadline;

7. reading, evaluating, and ranking proposals (by a panel of reviewers);

8. deciding which proposals will receive funding (by a panel of reviewers);

9. notifying applicants regarding the award;

10. negotiating the nature and extent of the award;

11. celebrating the resulting agreement (e.g., publicizing award to profession and community);

12. implementing the program;

13. performing the formative and summative program evaluation;

14. submitting required programmatic and financial reports to the funding source in accordance with mutually agreed-upon deadlines;

15. (where applicable) submitting an application for continuance funds.

Table 1-1 provides a means of visualizing the planning process.

Table 1-1

Grant Development Flowchart

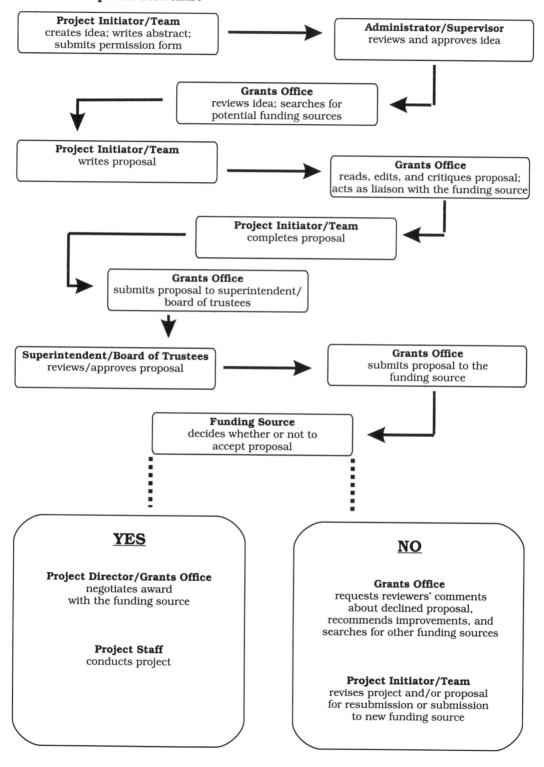

Project Initiator/Team
creates idea; writes abstract;
submits permission form

Administrator/Supervisor
reviews and approves idea

Grants Office
reviews idea; searches for
potential funding sources

Project Initiator/Team
writes proposal

Grants Office
reads, edits, and critiques proposal;
acts as liaison with the funding source

Project Initiator/Team
completes proposal

Grants Office
submits proposal to superintendent/
board of trustees

Superintendent/Board of Trustees
reviews/approves proposal

Grants Office
submits proposal to the
funding source

Funding Source
decides whether or not to
accept proposal

YES

Project Director/Grants Office
negotiates award
with the funding source

Project Staff
conducts project

NO

Grants Office
requests reviewers' comments
about declined proposal,
recommends improvements, and
searches for other funding sources

Project Initiator/Team
revises project and/or proposal
for resubmission or submission
to new funding source

B.   The Rationale for Planning

Grantseeking is an ongoing process. The time frame required to develop innovative projects does not necessarily coincide with particular dates in the calendar year. Funders issue announcements and requests for proposals on an almost daily basis.

Traditionally, administrators in many organizations have tended to view grantseeking as peripheral to the job descriptions of their subordinates. Accorded such a low priority, the task of seeking and securing additional financing is conducted hastily, without adequate attention to planning concerns. Grant proposals prepared in such a manner are frequently declined in deference to applicants who present more inclusive plans for an award.

The steady decline in state and federal funding during the 1990s has encouraged many organizations to hire at least one individual who coordinates efforts to procure external funding. Such positions carry various titles, including grant writer, proposal development specialist, federal programs officer, development officer, grants and proposal development specialist, and grants administrator.

Regardless of the titles, the establishment of an office to identify funding sources, to prepare and coordinate the writing of proposals for consideration by potential funders, and to manage grant awards has become increasingly important to libraries and other educational institutions. An inability to access discretionary money from government agencies, foundations, private corporations, and other supporters can force a reduction of programs and services.

C.   Readiness for Planning

Once an organizational team is formed, grant project planning truly begins. An effective planning process is not always considered requisite; in fact, it may be ignored or underestimated by inexperienced grantseekers. Furthermore, the team's productivity may be limited if the level of support and commitment from within the organization is insufficient for the task at hand.

Organizational barriers can potentially contribute to the failure of a grant development team. The team must recognize and respond to a notable principle of behavior: Organization prevents reorganization. Organizational commitment to a successful grants program changes priorities. Time and resources must be allocated differently, and new systems and procedures must be implemented. Resistance by the organization to such changes should be anticipated. However, an effective grantseeking process that secures additional funding will usually convince leadership that the changes in question promote the vitality of the organization.

Because successful grantseeking is a collaborative process, individuals throughout the organization must be properly motivated. The following steps can help lay the foundation for a favorable climate:

1.   Encourage a high-level administrator to issue (or endorse) a policy statement indicating that grantseeking is an organizational priority.

2.   Provide the time, resources, personnel, and training needed by grant development teams.

3. Recognize and reward grant preparation activities within the organization. For instance, such participation should be a major factor when considering promotions and raises.

4. Employ in-house newsletters or letters from a key administrator to recognize the grant development team members for their efforts.

5. Share available grant announcements and awards with others in the organization. Enthusiasm is contagious.

6. Begin small and build. Select a core staff to act as in-house grant experts. As they achieve success, others will want to become involved.

When the grant development team designs a project that reflects an understanding of both the institutional mission (see Chapter 2) and employee motivators (e.g., achievement, recognition, responsibility), the potential for success increases significantly. A number of organizational characteristics should be considered as part of the effort to achieve a match between project and organizational objectives.

1.   Historical Commitment to Planning

In an organization with a history of effective planning, the grant development team will have access to a wide array of documentation to serve its needs. An absence of such materials indicates an insufficient commitment to planning. An unwillingness to hire a qualified individual to coordinate strategic planning, exclusively, further underscores a lack of commitment. A file cabinet filled with plans that have never been implemented is yet another danger sign. A reliance upon consultants and other external experts to write plans can contribute to failure; successful implementation efforts throughout an organization generally reflect the involvement—and ultimate endorsement—of staff members. For the grant development team to function effectively, planning must be an ongoing process at all levels in the organization.

2.   The Reward System for Staff Contributions

Successful organizations typically reward employees for their efforts, including diligent work and creative contributions to the problem-solving process. The absence of an organizational program to distribute recognition to deserving staff will compromise employee efforts, generally, as well as grantseeking activities, specifically. Though some employees are highly self-motivated, the majority of workers require additional encouragement through a wide variety of mechanisms, including administrative recognition; greater influence within the organization, conferred by an increase in status and responsibilities; time-off provisions, sometimes in the form of flextime, which allow staff to share more time with family, pursue hobbies, and fulfill the demands of life; access to and support for special training opportunities, which increase employee skills and marketability within the workplace; increases in salary and fringe benefits; and perks, such as a liberal dress code, access to recreational facilities, and improvements in the work environment (e.g., background music).

3. Culture, Size, and Complexity of the Organization

An organization's culture reflects its shared beliefs. The members of an organization articulate their collective service philosophy through a mission statement. To transform this vision into reality, collective energies must be focused on the delivery of programs and services. Regardless of an organization's size or complexity, the mission statement functions as a cornerstone of the proposal development process. Initiatives designed to secure funding for programs and services that correlate directly to the mission statement merit primary consideration.

Nevertheless, size and complexity affect the determination of organizational priorities. Larger organizations have the resources required to offer more extensive arrays of programs and services, and can employ larger numbers of administrators to supervise specific activities. Smaller organizations often have fewer resources, and are likely to employ fewer administrators. More critical to a grant development process than size or complexity, though, is administrative support. When the planning phase for a grant proposal begins, each administrator should be invited and encouraged to participate. It is essential that the grant development team focus on the mission statement rather than rank-and-file departmental or program activities.

4. Rate of Growth

An organization experiencing rapid growth tends to focus its attention on the management of expansion. When the growth occurs outside the organization's span of control (e.g., a population explosion caused by the influx of new residents), administrators will feel pressured to redistribute resources that otherwise would have been available to the grant development team. If a pronounced rate of growth occurs within the organization itself, the need for controlled expansion increases. While the organization is expanding, the appropriate administrators should be expanding the internal capacity to accommodate increased planning and grant development activities. Regardless of the rate of growth, a grant development team aspiring to design projects reflecting both institutional needs and client services must thoroughly understand the organizational climate.

5. Financial Resources

The grant development process incurs costs that the applicant organization must underwrite. Costs typically include staff salaries and benefits, office space, equipment purchase and use, photocopying, communications (e.g., telephone, fax, Internet access), travel to "best practices" sites, and attendance at meetings with partner organizations. Though such preparatory expenses can be shared if the project includes partner organizations, funding agencies themselves do not underwrite grant development. This fact may not pose a serious problem for less ambitious activities, but more comprehensive projects encompassing considerable collaborative efforts across a geographically dispersed area can easily cost several thousand dollars.

The grant development team leader should negotiate a level of organizational support sufficient to complete the proposal writing process. During the initial stages of the planning phase, team members should identify all anticipated proposal development costs. The team leader should compile the projected expenses and forward them to the appropriate administrator.

If the organization cannot underwrite anticipated costs, the project might be salvaged by requesting team members to selectively modify proposed activities. However, encouraging grant development personnel to work without adequate financial support affects the integrity of the project and is an unsound management practice. Many experts advocate termination of grant development if an organization cannot support the process.

6. Access and Availability of Information

The proposal development process requires access to a minimum of two types of information. First, the team will need comprehensive background data describing the applicant organization, including history, grant management experience, and programs and services. As this information is compiled, it should be organized for optimum reference access. Relevant new and revised documents should be added to the reference (or "record") set. When these reference documents are properly maintained, the organizational data can be used in the development of every proposal.

The second type of required information includes research findings, "best practices," and other material relevant to the proposal. In the competitive environment characterizing grantsmanship today, development team members require access to vast amounts of up-to-date information. Resources available on the Internet (see Appendix A) are essential for maintaining currency with other grant-seeking institutions, newly released RFPs, research findings, grantsmanship training sessions, and "best practices." The power of the personal computer—coupled with two-way access to such resources as library collections, electronic (full-text) publications, model sites, and researchers and other experts (using e-mail)—provides instantaneous access to virtually any information, anywhere in the world. Commercial vendor services (e.g., DIALOG, Maxwell, Mead-Data's LEXIS/NEXIS) offering hundreds of exhaustive bibliographic, full-text, and numeric databases can be accessed through subscription on the Internet.

To effectively use these resources, team members must be able to use the Internet proficiently. Attaining a knowledge of available resources as well as a mastery of search techniques requires considerable time and effort. If no member of the team possesses a familiarity with or direct access to the Internet, someone who does should be recruited.

7. Willingness to Take Risks

Generally, funding agencies do not financially support routine, ongoing activities. Organizations lacking commitment to change and willingness to take risks are not likely to achieve success in the grantsmanship arena, though historically, many organizations have built enviable reputations through the permanency of their programs and services.

The decision to maintain a conservative stance is appropriate to some organizations. However, a dynamic, external environment has motivated many administrators to use various self-assessment tools for ensuring the continued vitality of their organizations well into the twenty-first century. These institutional studies frequently reflect a mandate for change. In organizations that use them, the grant development team has the responsibility and support to incorporate this commitment to change into its proposals.

Organizational self-assessment might be conducted using an instrument such as Table 1-2.

Table 1-2

Organizational Self-Assessment Tool

To determine your organization's strengths and weaknesses, check the box between each pair of descriptors that best reflects your assessment of the following:

Market share:	High	❑	❑	❑	❑	❑	Low
Market share:	Increasing	❑	❑	❑	❑	❑	Decreasing
Market position:	Protected	❑	❑	❑	❑	❑	Unprotected
Market pricing:	Leader	❑	❑	❑	❑	❑	Follower
Response capability:	Rapid	❑	❑	❑	❑	❑	Slow
Response capacity:	Broad	❑	❑	❑	❑	❑	Narrow
Name recognition:	High	❑	❑	❑	❑	❑	Low
Procurement costs:	Low	❑	❑	❑	❑	❑	High
Distribution costs:	Low	❑	❑	❑	❑	❑	High
Capacity usage:	High	❑	❑	❑	❑	❑	Low
Agency infrastructure:	Strong	❑	❑	❑	❑	❑	Weak
Agency operations:	Prosperous	❑	❑	❑	❑	❑	Unsuccessful
Access to capital:	High	❑	❑	❑	❑	❑	Low
Access to agency facilities:	Expandable	❑	❑	❑	❑	❑	Restrictive
Agency expertise:	High	❑	❑	❑	❑	❑	Low
Portfolio adaptability:	Great	❑	❑	❑	❑	❑	Little
Client relations:	Good	❑	❑	❑	❑	❑	Poor
Agency management:	Effective	❑	❑	❑	❑	❑	Ineffective
Client base:	Large	❑	❑	❑	❑	❑	Limited
Agency reputation:	Ethical	❑	❑	❑	❑	❑	Unethical
Recruitment potential:	Good	❑	❑	❑	❑	❑	Poor
Labor relations:	Good	❑	❑	❑	❑	❑	Poor
Services packaging:	Good	❑	❑	❑	❑	❑	Poor

Summarize organizational strengths and weaknesses.

Based upon the above assessment of organizational strengths and weak-nesses, consider the following opportunities for expansion. Indicate to what extent you could:

Provide new services for existing markets: Great ❑ ❑ ❑ ❑ ❑ Little

Provide new services for new markets: Great ❑ ❑ ❑ ❑ ❑ Little

Enter new markets providing existing services: Great ❑ ❑ ❑ ❑ ❑ Little

Increase current market penetration: Great ❑ ❑ ❑ ❑ ❑ Little

Improve existing technology: Great ❑ ❑ ❑ ❑ ❑ Little

Adopt new technology: Great ❑ ❑ ❑ ❑ ❑ Little

Differentiate services: Great ❑ ❑ ❑ ❑ ❑ Little

Provide excess capacity to others: Great ❑ ❑ ❑ ❑ ❑ Little

Acquire related or unrelated businesses: Great ❑ ❑ ❑ ❑ ❑ Little

Enter coalitions or affiliations: Great ❑ ❑ ❑ ❑ ❑ Little

Use personnel more effectively: Great ❑ ❑ ❑ ❑ ❑ Little

Based on the above assessments, summarize your organization's strengths:

_____

_____

D.   General Guidelines for the Pre-Development Planning Process

All administrators should be encouraged to participate in the ongoing review of organizational funding opportunities. Administrative involvement can motivate other personnel within their respective areas, thereby diminishing the possibility of overlooking viable funding sources and heightening the general interest in grant development. The participation of administrators who supervise programs focusing on key target groups (e.g., special education, early childhood education, library technology) should be particularly encouraged. All staff, as well, should be encouraged to explore external funding sources. The grant development team should investigate any promising sources identified by administrators and staff.

Information regarding potential funders is available primarily in two formats: electronic (particularly the Internet) and print databases. The latter format includes periodicals, newsletters, documents, and subscription services that distribute regular announcements of upcoming grant opportunities. An annotated guide to both formats is included in Appendix A.

Once potential funding sources have been identified, the grant development team should directly request any relevant formal announcements. These announcements customarily contain proposal guidelines, eligibility and program requirements, and required submission forms. Copies of the announcements should be shared within the team and with administrators.

Only obtainable grant monies should be pursued. Administrators should consider the following issues when determining the appropriateness of a funding source:

- The organization must be an eligible applicant as defined by the funding source.

- The project requirements must be acceptable within the context of the organization's mission.

- When matching funds are required, the organization must be capable of raising them.

If the source appears promising, the team should explore the level of interest in developing a particular grant project. Input should be solicited and encouraged from all sectors of the organization at this fact-finding stage of the process.

Securing an organizational commitment requires bridging the gap between a general interest in grantseeking and a specific conceptual design for the proposed project. Because conceptual design requires significant time and effort, the grant development process must be approached as an innovative opportunity to serve the community and meet its needs. A proposal involves many seemingly disparate parts; therefore, the crafting of a coherent document cannot be accomplished without envisioning the grant development process as a whole.

E.   Calendar Development

A calendar of key stages in the grant development process must be compiled early in the planning phase. The preparation of the calendar enables team members to adjust scheduling, coordinate personal activities, and conduct related research in a manner that optimizes their grantseeking efforts. A sample calendar appears in Table 1-3.

An effective approach to constructing the proposal development calendar is to begin with the deadline for submitting the proposal to the funding agency. Working backwards chronologically from this date, key stages should be identified and included in the calendar, allowing an adequate time frame for conducting each activity. Table 1-4, page 12, can help expedite the calendar preparation process.

Table 1-3

Proposal Development Calendar

Key Dates

February 5–9:	Appoint team members
February 12–16:	Share deliberations of proposal team with colleagues (potential advisors)
February 19–23:	Gather and share data
February 26–March 1:	Compile resources and write proposal
March 4–8:	Final review and edit
March 11–15:	Spring break
March 14:	Last day to submit proposal

Potential Calendar Problems

Coordination of tasks with partner organizations.

Deadline is near the end of spring break.

Administrative review and approval requires time.

Possible Solutions

Decide whether or not to proceed. Is enough time available? Delegate tasks to a small group to expedite completion.

Present modified calendar to potential team members and partner organizations.

Schedule after-school and weekend sessions.

Solicit administrative support for after-school and weekend sessions (if needed).

Table 1-4

Proposal Development Summary

Funding agency:

Project deadline:

Delivery mode:

Preliminary project title:

Project goal:

Project abstract:

Project time line—Starting date:

Ending date:

Project management—Director name:

Job title:

Telephone:

Fax:

E-mail address:

Review process—Review team members:

Draft review date:

Budgeting process—Team members:

Finance officer/staff review:

Budget review date:

Approval process—Administrator(s):

Board meeting date:

The number of copies required and method of delivery (to the funding agency) are important considerations when preparing the proposal development calendar. Pickup and delivery schedules for major carriers (e.g., U.S. Postal Service, Federal Express, United Parcel Service) must be researched, including their overnight and priority services. When applicable, the holiday delays should also be considered. It is advisable to designate the individual who will be responsible for arranging carrier pickup or taking the package to a drop-off point prior to the deadline.

Proposal writing is a complex, time-consuming process. However, it can be simplified and shorn of wasteful tasks when divided into manageable components. The team must understand that time management is the central concern of grant-seeking. Team members can best use the time available by adopting a number of proven strategies:

- Enjoy the process. Individuals who dislike proposal development—or, more specifically, a particular delegated task—are unlikely to devote more than the minimum time necessary to fulfill their responsibilities. Consequently, the team is unlikely to realize its potential.

- Recognize that there is always time for important tasks. All professionals are prone to a wide array of distractions, but those who order their priorities and focus their efforts accordingly tend to achieve greater success.

- Identify and allot time for high-priority tasks. Because all tasks should fulfill a key role in the proposal, the priority status accorded a particular task will vary based upon the current stage of development.

- Write ideas on index cards. Many good ideas are lost if not recorded. Documenting and organizing ideas for future use can save time in the planning process.

- Recall long-term goals while performing small tasks. All tasks should, incrementally, expedite accomplishment of the team's major goals. Tasks that do not fit this pattern should be promptly discarded.

- Set priorities daily. The execution of key tasks does not always occur as planned. To accommodate dynamic adjustments to the project agenda, a flexible approach must be maintained.

- Do first things first. The accomplishment of each goal is built upon a sequence of tasks; the sequential process ensures integrity of the final product. Failure to properly execute a particular stage of the process will undermine effectiveness in executing tasks at a later stage.

- Eliminate unproductive tasks. Tasks that fail to advance the project may not be perceived as unproductive during the initial planning process. They are typically retained because of their value in past projects, or because of the comfort level associated with continuing to execute them. Eliminating tasks that lack value increases time for more productive activities.

- Delegate whenever possible. Teams are typically assembled to create an efficient combination of individual skills and capabilities. Members should focus on only the tasks for which they are most qualified—or have been specifically selected—to execute. If the team lacks particular competencies, external experts should be recruited or contracted to meet these needs.

- Focus on one task at a time. Attempts to execute two or more tasks simultaneously are likely to dilute effectiveness.

- Use computers for communication. To ensure that project goals are achieved within the specified time frame, effective communication among team members is essential when orchestrating tasks. Geographic dispersal of project participants, combined with scheduling considerations, can severely limit meeting opportunities. Whereas typewritten memos and newsletters were used for efficiency in the past, most grant development teams today find e-mail and documents generated by word processing software to be the most inexpensive and timely forms of communication.

- Establish deadlines for team members. Target dates for the completion of all tasks will help the team maintain the schedule for submitting an on-time proposal. Failure to meet particular deadlines will alert the project head to the need for adjusting the calendar.

- Handle each piece of paper only once. An unnecessarily repetitious process causes duplication of effort. An explicit plan concerning job responsibilities and the flow of information will minimize this problem.

- Organize records and resources. Duplication of effort also results from replacing key documents or information that team members cannot locate. Files of both physical materials and electronic resources should be subjected to a useful form of authority control, and updated regularly. Records management policies (particularly regarding the retention of files) can be extremely helpful in facilitating effective organizational access to information. When necessary, hire support staff to handle the routine tasks of records management.

- Anticipate the unanticipated. Regardless of the team's resolve to follow the calendar, unexpected tasks and delays in the grant development process are inevitable. Success is most likely when team members avoid morale problems and employ a constructive approach to problem solving. Experienced grantseeking teams typically allow an additional week at the end of the process to accommodate unexpected tasks and delays. Without this cushion, the final days can become frantic.

F. Planning Meetings

1. Initial Planning Meeting

Once the preliminary decision to proceed has been made, the first planning meeting should be held. Representatives from each participating unit (e.g., school campuses, branch libraries) should not only be invited but encouraged to attend. Representatives at this meeting should begin by appointing the proposal development team. Those present may decide that they will serve as the team, or they may invite others with particular expertise to augment their group.

Once participants have been appointed, the team is ready to select a facilitator (or chairperson). The choice must be carefully deliberated because this individual will be responsible for scheduling and coordinating all proposal development activities. The traditional practice has been to select the individual with the highest-ranking title and function in the organization. However, this approach does not guarantee a facilitator who understands the programmatic focus of proposal development, nor a willingness to participate in the process. Prior success in securing grant funding and motivating committees within the organization should be given top priority in selecting the team facilitator.

The facilitator will ultimately deliver the completed proposal to the organization's chief administrator (i.e., superintendent for a public school district, director for a public library). The facilitator must establish effective communication channels with all administrators who will sign the formal letter required for proposal submission to the funder and then recommend approval of the document by the organization's governing body (i.e., board of directors for a public school district, board of trustees for a public library).

Next, the team should assess the potential funding source for alignment with the organization's mission, services, and activities. To this end, team members should review funding agency documents. For schools, this process will include assessing the degree of confluence between the funder and both state and federal department of education priorities and initiatives. For public libraries, the source must also be assessed for accordance with regional system services, state library programs, and relevant federal mandates. Table 1-5, page 16, can assist in this review process.

In cases where the potential funder is deemed inappropriate, the team would be well advised to move immediately to the search for other possible funding sources. Grant donors are extremely wary of grantseeking organizations that attempt to forge the appearance of compatible objectives and activities on paper, when in fact, the two entities have little in common.

A calendar of key dates in the proposal development process should be distributed and discussed during the initial planning meeting. The team should then decide upon the frequency and duration of future meetings, and modify the calendar as necessary. The modified calendar should be distributed to all team members and administrators, including those from partner organizations. A compilation of the names, mail and e-mail addresses, and telephone/fax/e-mail numbers of all team members should also be distributed. Attendance at future meetings will be maximum if reminders are sent to each member through the preferred channel (e.g., mail, e-mail, fax).

Table 1-5

Proposal Development Problem Analysis

State the problem:

Student population (check all that apply):

Gender:

    ❑ male

    ❑ female

Ethnicity:

    ❑ Caucasian

    ❑ Hispanic

    ❑ African American

    ❑ Native American

    ❑ Asian American

    ❑ Other

Socioeconomic factors:

    ❑ "at risk"

    ❑ ESL/bilingual

    ❑ limited English proficiency

    ❑ Chapter I

    ❑ special education

    ❑ free/reduced lunch

Geographic area affected (supply data):

City:

County:

Census tract:

Other designation(s):

The facilitator should attempt to secure a consensus regarding noteworthy proposal issues, including funding agency requirements, technical specifications that must be developed and included, the evaluation plan, and budget breakdowns. The initial planning meeting is also the appropriate time to consider the reporting requirements for programmatic and financial aspects of the project, as well as the resources necessary to fulfill these requirements. Above all, the team must reach a consensus on the assignment of responsibilities and task completion dates. A comparative analysis of the skills of each member is a necessary condition for defining individual roles.

2.   Conceptual Design Meeting

The second proposal development meeting should focus on developing a conceptual design for the project. Until the team reaches a consensus regarding this design, its efforts are likely to remain ineffectual at best. A group review of pertinent data concerning the organization's mission, services, and activities will enable the team to identify components and objectives that should receive major attention in the proposed project. Table 1-6 can assist the team in this process.

Table 1-6

Identifying Project Components and Objectives

Project component:

Project objective I:

 Major activities:

Project objective II:

 Major activities:

Project objective III:

 Major activities:

Major problems/barriers:

G. Decisions Relating to Proposal Preparation

During the preliminary planning phase of a project, the team should make a number of decisions relating to the writing, editing, and formatting of the proposal. These decisions are largely concerned with role and task assignments, and will reduce the likelihood of misunderstandings among team members during proposal development.

1. Writing and Editing Issues

Team members must make two critical decisions regarding the writing and editing phases: Who will write the narrative portion of the proposal? Who will edit the final document prior to printing and submitting it to the funding agency? Each of these tasks can be delegated to either a single person or a small committee (usually a subgroup of the grant development team). Experienced grantseekers vary in their opinions as to which approach is best, but either can be successful.

The team facilitator (or chairperson) and team members should discuss their preferences. If any team members withhold their preferences, conflict is likely to occur during the proposal development process. If the conflict arises at a critical stage, valuable resources may be diverted from the collaborative effort, and a weak proposal may result. Worse, the team could become dysfunctional and fail to complete the proposal.

When the team is fortunate enough to include a number of proficient writers, a joint writing committee may be the best option, assuming that appointed team members are willing to invest the time and effort required. Team members better suited for conceptual development and specific technical aspects of the project (e.g., technology, staff training and development, evaluation design), though, may feel uncomfortable writing a portion of the narrative.

When a number of individuals contribute to writing a single document, the final product tends to read unevenly. Changes in writing style may be not only obvious, but annoying. Without a seamless presentation, the proposal is unlikely to secure funding. Generally, this dilemma must be directly addressed in the selection of an editor (or joint editing committee) as well as the establishment of editing procedures.

If the team decides against a joint writing committee, they must select an individual writer. Appointing a skilled writer will help ensure a consistent writing style. To ensure a coherent proposal, the writer should meet continually with team members to discuss the proposed project. The writer must have excellent listening skills, and must be able to understand and convey the spirit and intent of each member's contributions. Because the proposal will inevitably reflect the writer's personal understanding of the project, the initial drafts should be reviewed by team members who can capably articulate the project's technical components.

The editing task poses similar challenges to the team. When the team includes a number of proficient writers, a joint editing committee may be the best option. Carefully consider the potential contributions of each individual before deciding upon the team editing strategy. Because disagreements about wording, punctuation, and format are likely, the editing team must establish a process for reaching consensus.

If the team decides against a joint editing committee, they must select an individual editor. Because this individual will exercise considerable control over the final document, the editor must be not only an objective reader, but a capable writer who can articulate the project and its components. Above all, the editor should not be the same individual who wrote the proposal.

Less experienced teams have a tendency to select as editor an English teacher or an individual who majored in English in college. Though this approach might seem logical, selecting a team member who possesses the skills and experience specific to proposal writing is a better approach. Proposals require a special type of writing; ability (including editorial ability) in other forms of writing does not necessarily transfer to the proposal genre.

2.   Document Formatting Issues

Because of the proportion of effort devoted to writing the narrative, grant development teams typically do not focus sufficient attention on the layout of the document. Although review of a proposal in a competitive environment tends to be concentrated on content rather than layout, proper attention to the latter (especially to funder's specific formatting requirements—e.g., pagination, spacing, margins, length of text, use of particular highlighting devices) can mean the difference between success and failure. Therefore, the team should consider formatting issues throughout the entire proposal development process.

Experienced grant writers are likely to recognize the inherent advantages of using word processing and desktop publishing software to prepare proposals. Such software enables the grant writer to work efficiently, and enables on-demand printing of document drafts for review and comment by team members. If the preliminary drafts are prepared using such software, the formatting specifications for the final document can be incorporated with minimal effort.

No matter what type of platform (e.g., IBM-compatible, Apple Macintosh) is used in preparing the proposal, all team members involved in the tasks of writing and editing should use the same software (and the same version of the software). The team should select the software during initial planning of the proposal development process. Use of the same software allows the team to assemble the overall document with minimal effort and without file conversion.

Some team members may choose to prepare a document draft in typewritten or handwritten form. If so, the team must designate an individual to transfer the material to a file in the chosen software. Because writing skills are a premium commodity in proposal writing, do not discourage proficient writers solely because they wish to prepare their portion of the document in an alternative manner.

Table 1-7

Steps in Conceptual Design of the Project

1.   Understand the Problem

Identify the problem in terms of client conditions ensuing from the absence of knowledge or skills, or from a particular social difficulty. Review available data and assess contributing factors and root causes. An effective solution to the problem requires a thorough analysis of the problem.

2.   Brainstorm Solutions

Success in brainstorming solutions involves the following intangible skills:

- Listening

- Observing

- Sensing community enthusiasm and support

- Trusting personal intuition about the viability of project ideas

The key is allowing oneself the freedom to think and innovate without self-inhibition. Avoid confinement to past ways of addressing the problem.

Focus on the underlying or unifying aspects of ideas, and combine these aspects with the recurring themes expressed by others attempting to solve the same problem. Integrate the model derived from these ideas with the practical considerations emerging from the organizational, community, and funder sectors. The solution will undergo continued modification as it is examined from each perspective.

Organizational Perspective

Applying the organizational perspective requires acquisition of the following background information:

- History and mission statement

- Service area (in geographic terms)

- Population served

- Current programs

- Current staffing (e.g., workload, interests, relationships, qualifications)

- Future plans

- Funding sources (percent of total budget of each)

- Other organizations providing similar services

Consider whether the organization possesses the competency, connections, and staff capabilities to conduct the proposed project. In determining the organization's capability to manage projects, begin by analyzing its past performance record:

- What types of projects have been successfully managed?

- What types of projects have been difficult to manage?

- Identify the majority of the organization's contacts

A cooperative project may be necessary in response to one or more of three areas of pressure:

1. Diminishing financial resources

2. Increasing magnitude of social problems

3. A need to increase efficiency of service delivery and reduce social problems

Relationships among organizations tend to be fragile in nature, requiring a heightened political awareness. An attempt to implement a project that is currently being implemented by another organization in the field may encounter obstacles. The threatened organization may manipulate public opinion to neutralize such a move. However, such competition can be healthy when one of the following factors applies:

- A project is copied or duplicated because it serves a different target group.

- The encroaching organization possesses the technology to improve the service.

- The encroaching organization will provide the service more effectively.

Competition for limited funding among organizations within a comparatively small geographic area, though, is likely to be counterproductive. If the need cannot be met with a new approach, a cooperative project may be the only viable option.

Community Perspective

Central to understanding a problem is the ability to ascertain the readiness of the community to address it. The solution an organization hopes to achieve requires a certain critical mass of community support.

(Table 1-7 continues on page 22.)

Table 1-7—Continued

Funder Perspective

At this point, a grant proposal team should begin identifying potential funders. The availability of grant money will often stimulate an emphasis on particular aspects of the proposed project. Although positioning oneself to take advantage of funding opportunities is wise, grantseekers should be wary of modifying the focus of the project to the extent that the organization takes a direction that is ill suited to its overall mission. A satisfactory compromise between the grantseeker's vision and the funder's perspective is most likely to be reached when the grantseeker clearly understands the funder's perspective. Funders prefer proposals that fit within the mission or guidelines they have developed to direct their funding activities, proposals that come from organizations enjoying strong community support and a reputation for achieving goals, and proposals that will reflect them favorably.

3.   Identify Solutions

From the pool of brainstormed solutions, select the ones deemed most promising. Include a rationale for these choices. The following questions can guide the evaluation of solutions:

Does the solution fit within the mission of the organization?   ❏ Y   ❏ N

Does the solution address aspects of community need?   ❏ Y   ❏ N

Can need for the solution be documented?   ❏ Y   ❏ N

Does the solution have a well-defined target group?   ❏ Y   ❏ N

Is the scope of the solution realistic for the organization?
    (Consider staffing, physical facilities, and experience.)   ❏ Y   ❏ N

How does the solution compare to efforts by other
    organizations to address the need?   ❏ Y   ❏ N

Does the solution incite support from the organization's
    chief administrator?   ❏ Y   ❏ N

Will the clients embrace and benefit from the solution?   ❏ Y   ❏ N

Does the solution meet the needs of the funder?
    (Is it an effective use of grant funds?)   ❏ Y   ❏ N

Does the solution enhance and support future
    development of the organization?   ❏ Y   ❏ N

Team members must be sensitive to cultural differences and perceptions related to addressing the problem so that the will or needs of one group are not imposed upon another. Questions about the ethics of the solution might include:

- Is the need the solution will address recognized by the client as a need?

- Is there any chance that clients will be coerced into accepting the solution?

- Is there any chance that the solution will adversely affect its target group's status in the community?

- Does the solution impose particular values on the target group other than its own?

4.   Describe Expected Results and Benefits

Project the changes likely to occur, and whom will be affected, as a result of conducting the project. Attempt to describe the benefits from the client's perspective in terms of changes in the following:

- knowledge, attitudes, beliefs

- the acquisition of skills

- physical, economic, or social condition

- the environment

Also, try to ascertain whether there will be a single benefit or multiple benefits for the target group.

5.   Determine Tasks to Accomplish Solutions

Also referred to as implementation procedures, project activities, or methodologies, these tasks concern the preparation for delivery of the solution and the eventual accomplishment of the solution. They include the following:

- recruitment of project staff

- materials development

- implementation of public relations activities

- scheduling of training sessions, workshops, etc.

- publication of newsletters

(Table 1-7 continues on page 24.)

Table 1-7—Continued

6. Identify Necessary Resources and Estimate Project Expenses

The resources necessary to conduct project tasks include nonpersonnel items as well as personnel:

- staff
- volunteers
- office supplies
- equipment
- facilities

Itemization of these resources allows a general estimate of project expenses.

7. Reassess Capacity of Solutions

Determine whether or not the solutions adequately address the need. The data derived from prior steps may demand modification of proposed solutions, or reconsideration of other solutions. Discussing problems with other staff may assist in realigning perspectives.

8. Reassess Efficacy of Tasks

Determine whether or not the tasks adequately facilitate the desired outcome. The tasks must ensure that appropriate service is delivered to clients.

9. Identify Evaluation Methods

Identify the criteria and data collection methods that will be used to determine whether or not the desired outcome has been achieved. For instance, in attempting to measure change in knowledge in the target group, pretesting and posttesting strategies (e.g., written and verbal tests) might be used.

2
Project Design

If the grant development team has thoroughly planned the grant proposal, a fundamentally sound project design is likely to follow. Project design begins with consensus building—for a mission statement, a project goal, and related objectives and activities. The team should take whatever time is needed to acclimate itself to this process. Many grantseeking groups have a tendency to rush into the design stage without first arriving at a clearly defined need and projected solutions. The result can be a disjointed array of ideas that poorly fulfill client needs.

The recent experience of a grant development team pursuing a U.S. Department of Education "Challenge Grant in Technology" illustrates the problems ensuing from a lack of cohesive effort. The representatives of 18 partner institutions met weekly for three months to discuss and plot a course of action. Divided into various committees to focus on specific issues, team members preoccupied themselves with hidden agendas rather than collaborative decision making. Based upon the existing feedback and the prepared timetable, the chairperson concluded that progress was lagging. Despite the chair's repeated attempts to refocus team efforts around a single mission statement, the participants maintained their rigid postures on a host of issues, such as proposed services for students, faculty, and parents; involvement with emerging and experimental technologies; equipment to be acquired for pilot sites; and professional development frameworks. As a result, the chair convened the team, thanked them for their efforts, compiled existing notes and recommendations, and continued the effort alone, concentrating on project components for which consensus had been reached. Because of the breakdown of collaborative decision making, the final document reflected little of the expertise possessed by individual team members. The proposal was not funded.

A scenario of this type can be avoided. If all members of the team thoroughly understand the overall emphasis of the project, the design process—and ensuing implementation of the project—can proceed smoothly.

A.   The Importance of a Lucid Mission Statement

A mission statement outlines the grant development team's vision of the organization upon successful implementation of the proposed project. A lucid mission statement requires considerable forethought. Inexperience or lack of effort often leads to a restatement of funding agency requirements. Though a restatement may convey an understanding of the requirements for serious consideration for an award, it may not reflect the applicant organization or the project. If the mission statement does not indicate an understanding of the proposed project within the context of both the organization's and the funder's operational goals, the proposal is unlikely to secure an award.

From an internal perspective, failure to write an adequate mission statement may result in wasteful expenditure of valuable resources and a continued lack of focus on the part of the grant development team. Reaching team consensus for a workable mission statement is the preliminary step in project design.

B.   Project Goal Development

The project goal articulates the mission statement and is the single most important component of the grant proposal. Lack of a well-stated goal indicates a weak, disorganized planning effort. Rather than an appropriate goal statement, many grant development teams merely prepare a brief statement indicating the project to be implemented, the equipment to be purchased, or the new services to be introduced. Though these considerations are important components of the grant proposal, they typically relate to project objectives and activities, and are no substitute for a project goal.

When developing a project goal, team members should consider 1) the legislative authority that empowers a government agency to fund projects with discretionary dollars, 2) the environment in which they work, and 3) the population the proposed project will benefit. Government agencies usually state the legislative authority in their requests for proposals (RFPs) and requests for applications (RFAs). The Library Services and Construction Act (LSCA)—instituted in 1964 as an expansion of the Library Services Act (1956) and modified in 1997— is the federal legislation with which school and public libraries are most likely to be familiar. LSCA has mandated the support of a variety of projects through its sections (titles), most notably innovative services, construction, and interinstitutional cooperation. LSCA funding has been available either directly from the agency source or through state libraries.

Though all LSCA title allotments are governed by federal legislation, some have been redefined through various state processes and regulations. These changes reflect a concerted effort by various library—and other educational—agencies to tailor the LSCA to better fit their respective service environments. For example, in California, LSCA guidelines have been modified to include the following:

- Bringing library service to areas and to populations without services.

- Improving library service to areas and populations with inadequate services.

- Providing library services to disadvantaged persons, which includes low income, English-speaking minority cultures—such as African-American and Native-American groups—and other least-served populations.

- Providing library service to physically handicapped persons.

- Providing library service to persons in state institutions.

- Supporting Major Urban Resource Libraries.

- Supporting National or Regional Resource Centers.

- Providing library service to persons of limited English-speaking ability.

- Providing services to the elderly.

- Providing Community Information Referral Centers.

- Providing literacy programs.

- Providing intergenerational library programs.

- Providing childcare center library programs.

- Providing library literacy centers.

- Providing drug abuse prevention programs.

The team should obtain the LSCA handbook for their state, which is prepared and distributed by the state library. Reading RFPs, RFAs, state guidelines for administering grant monies, and other documentation provides insight into the factors likely to receive the highest consideration by proposal reviewers. Proposals that respond to stated priorities have a significantly greater chance to secure funding.

An effective goal statement is often difficult to write. To produce a succinct statement, the grant development team should choose its words carefully. The most convincing, powerful goal statements are often written in the past tense and contain action verbs. However, effective goal statements can also be written in the present and future tenses. Table 2-1 is an inventory of frequently used action verbs, compiled by Donald Orlich and Patricia Orlich in *The Art of Writing Successful R&D Proposals*.

Table 2-1

Action Verbs Frequently Used in Goal Statements

apply	examine	purchase
assemble	feed	reclaim
assess	identify	reduce
build	illustrate	regulate
classify	implement	repair
compare	increase	review
conduct	install	select
demonstrate	observe	synthesize
design	plan	test
determine	prepare	train
develop	produce	transport
evaluate	provide	validate

A simple declaration (e.g., "The purpose of this project is to . . .") generally is effective in conveying the goal without confusing or misleading the reader. If the goal cannot be written as a single sentence that succinctly indicates what is to be accomplished, the team should reconsider the project's focus.

1.   Goal Development in Public School Districts

Public school district proposals should focus on serving student needs, improving academic achievement, enhancing instructional strategies, increasing parental involvement in the learning process, and increasing access to library resources (e.g., key print, multimedia, and Internet resources). Examples of project goals developed in public school districts are presented in Table 2-2.

Table 2-2

Example Project Goals—Public School Districts

To prevent drug use among young people in Grant City by promoting their educational, social, and emotional well-being.

To assist teachers and students in achieving computer literacy.

The grant development team must become familiar with the policies and public statements of the school district. These documents reflect the official vision of the district's governing body, the board of trustees. The team should acquire and read the recommendations and campus plans of all site-based decision-making teams in the district. These groups, composed of community representatives, assist in the overall governance of the district. Their collective efforts provide a blueprint of the district's educational environment.

2.   Goal Development in Public Libraries

Public library proposals should focus on the information needs of the community at large, most notably developing the workforce, improving economic and educational opportunities, and increasing access to a wide variety of media. Examples of project goals developed in public libraries are presented in Table 2-3.

Table 2-3

Example Project Goals—Public Libraries

To train public service staff to work effectively with the various multicultural, multiethnic populations in their community.

To provide essential business information to the entrepreneurs and unemployed, thereby promoting business retention and encouraging economic development.

The grant development team should obtain copies of all policy and procedural documents produced by the library board, all staff organizations, and Friends of the Library. Unless the contributions of all formal and informal groups comprising the public library's governance structure are represented, team members will likely develop an incomplete understanding of their target environment.

Substantial reductions in government spending in recent years have hindered the ability of public libraries to continue offering the programs and services necessary to meet the educational, cultural, and recreational needs of their communities. The dynamic growth of new information technologies has further complicated the efforts of public libraries to meet these needs. The availability of nontraditional funding sources offers a way for public libraries to overcome projected budgetary shortfalls. However, public libraries must exercise care in the targeting of funders whose expectations match community mandates.

C.   The Relationship Between the Project Goal Statement and Project Objectives

Project objectives provide elaboration of the project goal by dividing it into a series of desired outcomes. The following proposal excerpt illustrates the relationship between the project goal and a more focused set of objectives.

> Goal: This program is designed to prepare parents to function independently and effectively in helping their children develop to their own potentials.
>
> Objectives: The parents who participate in the program will be able to
>
> 1.   identify the education content in events that occur in the home;
>
> 2.   structure sequential and cumulative instructional tasks in the home for the child;
>
> 3.   observe the child and use checklists to monitor progress;
>
> 4.   use available equipment and processes in the home to teach children specific skills; and
>
> 5.   use packaged materials prepared by the project or library staff in teaching specific skills.

A set of objectives is the strategic core of the proposal. It specifies precisely what the project proposes to achieve, as well as what evidence will indicate project success for the target group. In other words, the objectives provide the basis for developing the evaluation criteria, because the former designate the latter. The following recommendations should be considered when developing a set of project objectives:

- Clearly describe the project's objectives, hypotheses, and research questions.

- Frame the objectives without burying them in a morass of narrative.

- Indicate why the objectives are significant and timely.

- Include objectives that *comprehensively* describe the intended outcomes of the project.

- Include objectives that are concisely written and easy to understand.

- Indicate how the objectives proceed logically from the needs statement and directly address the chosen problem.

- State the objectives, hypotheses, and research questions in such a way that they can be later evaluated or tested.

- Indicate why the objectives are appropriate and important to the funder.

- Indicate that the hypotheses rest on sufficient evidence and are conceptually sound.

- Justify how the objectives are manageable and feasible.

In the construction of objectives, use an infinitive phrase that specifies important factors of the action involved, such as **what** it will be, **whom** it will affect, and **why** it will occur. For example, the project objective "to implement the Gourmet TAAS Reading Curriculum to improve student proficiency in reading" specifies what the action will be (implementation of the Gourmet TAAS Reading Curriculum), whom the action will affect (students), and why the action will occur (to improve reading proficiency). This objective effectively communicates a major emphasis of the proposed project. In most cases, more interpretation or elaboration will be necessary to further focus the action of the objective (who will do it, when it will be done, how it will be done, etc.), but the objective should be no more than two sentences in length. Additional procedural information can be provided in the "project design" section of the proposal (see Chapter 3).

The following guidelines should also be considered when developing a set of objectives:

- List objectives in approximate order of importance, or in expected chronological order of achievement if submitting a phased proposal.

- Do not confuse objectives (ends) with methods (means). A good objective emphasizes what will be done and when it will be done, whereas a method will explain why or how it will be done.

- Keep the set of objectives relatively short in length; one-half page may prove sufficient.

- Use action verbs in the infinitive form (*to* + base verb), then complete the action and express it in measurable terms.

The essence of any proposal lies in the project objectives. Therefore, it should come as no surprise that a funding agency's rationale for rejecting a proposal is frequently related to problems within the set of project objectives. Typical problems include the following:

- The objectives are of limited significance. In many cases, proposals are simply not worthy of fiscal support. Donald Orlich and Patricia Orlich have noted that this situation poses special problems for the grant-seeking organization: Few individuals within the organization—or, more specifically, within the grant development team—will ever be courageous or honest enough to inform the proposal writer that the objectives are insignificant or trite.

- The objectives are nebulous, diffuse, or unclear.

- The objectives propose to accomplish more than the methods or budget will allow.

- The objectives are not clearly stated. In some cases, writers merely "talk around" an objective rather than stating it in explicit terms. In other cases, the objective reads as more of a global purposes than a specific, measurable, achievable outcome. The best solution to these flaws would be to use one of the following lead-ins to the set of objectives: "The objectives of this proposal are . . . ," or "The research objectives are. . . ." Such a device forces the writer to focus on what the project will accomplish.

- The objectives are unrealistic.

- The objectives are confusing, vague, unmeasurable, and clearly inappropriate to the purpose of the grant.

- The objectives state the problem rather than the outcomes that will result in a solution. As a result, the proposal communicates confusion between the condition and the intended solution.

- The objectives are vague and stated as "activities" or "procedures"— and are thus unmeasurable (e.g., a project concerned with determining student attitudes should contain a goal worded "to conduct a survey among students . . . ").

- The objectives are vague and difficult to measure (e.g., no targets are set in terms of faculty reached, trainees enrolled, disciplines involved, etc.). In some cases, the objectives contain imprecise terms. Donald Orlich and Patricia Orlich have stated that a number of proposals have included as an objective " . . . that the learning environment of the high school become more humanistic." This may well be a worthy ideal; however, as written, it is not a meaningful objective because it is vague and unmeasurable.

- Too many objectives are included. Proposal reviewers are likely to reject proposals that incorporate an unmanageable number of objectives. Also, the more objectives included, the greater the likelihood that proposal reviewers will find an objective they consider worthy of criticism.

Given the large number of possible pitfalls relating to the formulation of project objectives, this activity should receive special attention during the planning and proposal writing stages of the grant development process.

D. Conceptual Design of the Project

1. Preliminary Checklists

Once the goal statement has been written, the grant development team is ready to design the project and to identify specific objectives and activities. The team should consider the questions in Table 2-4 when forming ideas and exploring alternative approaches to achieving the identified goal.

Table 2-4

Project Design Checklist

Assessing the Need

- What is the target population?

- What is the need/problem of the target population?

- What are the causes of the need/problem?

- What are the major unresolved or unsolved issues regarding this need/problem?

- How can the need/problem be measured? What documentation is available to support the need/problem?

- What does the current literature in this area say about the problem/ need —national, state, and local—and approaches to solving/meeting it?

Defining the Project

- What goal does the project propose?

- What special approaches can be developed to achieve that goal?

- What alternative approaches can be used?

- What is unique or innovative about the project?

- What is significant about the project?

- What resources (from funder, district, community, etc.) will be necessary to conduct the project?

- What is the projected budget for conducting the project?

(Table 2-4 continues on page 34.)

Figure 2-4—Continued

Establishing an Organization's Qualifications

- What are the organization's goals?

- What previous experience (e.g., grant management experience) qualifies the organization to conduct the project?

- Does the organization have the capacity/resources to conduct the project?

- Who will be involved in the project—both internal and external collaborators? What are the qualifications of key personnel?

- Has the project team sought input from experts?

Conducting the Project

- What are the expected results of the project?

- Who will evaluate the project, and how?

- How will the project be continued after grant funding expires?

Before developing the conceptual design of a project, the team should address a number of questions relating to the organization's capability to conduct the proposed project, in addition to its capability to manage grant funds. Consideration of the questions in Table 2-5 will prepare the team for the task of formulating a statement of limitations by which to govern the project. According to Donald Orlich and Patricia Orlich, the limitations should address the extent of the project, groups or categories to be included, groups or categories to be excluded, conditions that could affect the results of the project, and assumptions made by the principal investigator (or key team members).

Table 2-5

Organizational Capability Checklist

Strategic Plan

- Does the project fit the organization's overall mission?

- Does the project have the support of the organization's administrators?

- Will the project receive the highest priority from the organization?

Resources

- What internal resources (e.g., computer lab, video equipment, etc.) are available for conducting the project?

- What internal resources are available for securing matching funds?

- What unique features of the organization (e.g., abilities, successes, awards, grant-funded projects, geographic location) give it a competitive advantage in proposing the project?

Collaboration and Support

- Are the necessary departments and offices within the organization able to collaborate in conducting the project?

- Can the organization collaborate with other organizations and institutions?

- Can support and endorsements for the project be gathered from external sources (e.g., the community, institutions of higher education, members of Congress)?

2.   Methodologies

The project design—commonly known as the methodology—essentially consists of a set of procedures for implementing the objectives to meet the need; in other words, it explains how the project will be conducted. The major types of methodologies include surveys, curriculum development or validation projects, staff development projects, case studies, and experimental studies. The first four types are often referred to as nonexperimental types.

Surveys, widely employed within the social sciences, are appropriate for collecting data regarding a particular trait or for documenting attitudes concerning a set of concepts, ideas, or programs. In addition to a set of objectives, its key components include a data collection instrument (e.g., personal interview schedules, questionnaires) and a sample of respondents. More specifically, the survey generally includes determining the purpose of the study, determining the target population, determining the method of investigation, determining the question format, writing and coding responses, planning the method of tabulation, planning the method of analysis, determining the sample population, writing a cover letter, pretesting the survey instrument, conducting the survey, accounting for returns, providing a follow-up for nonrespondents, processing returned data, analyzing returned data, compiling findings, displaying findings, making conclusions, and writing the final report. Surveys differ from experimental studies in that they attempt to measure opinions or a particular situation rather than manipulate variables.

Curriculum-related projects usually concern development or validation, or a combination of the two. Such projects typically include a statement of objectives, determination of the method of investigation, determination of the scope and sequence of learning experiences, description of content, delineation of procedures for evaluating the effectiveness of the curriculum, and preparation of some kind of product. Objectives are usually worded from the perspective of student learnings. In many cases, objectives focus on the behaviors that learners should exhibit as a result of implementing the curriculum, translated into criteria against which the curriculum is to be evaluated. In recent years, the federal government has made available many curriculum grants within the area of project adoption (i.e., the dissemination or implementation of already tested projects) as opposed to the accompanying areas of development and validation.

Staff development projects generally mirror curriculum designs, with the exception that the emphasis is to instill a selected staff with a set of competencies, instructional methods, curriculum techniques, or program skills. Donald Orlich and Patricia Orlich have argued that projects likely to appeal to funders would include the use of institutes to accomplish staff development tasks; external consultants to instruct a group of trainers selected from within the organization; institutions of higher education that offer specially designed workshops, courses, or seminars to meet predetermined staff needs; media as a method of disseminating new knowledge or skills; and self-instructional materials (e.g., programmed instruction, audiovisual tutorial systems).

Case studies are useful for gathering data and describing changes that may occur in individuals, organizations, or instructional techniques. They can be employed effectively only when the observation team possesses considerable knowledge about the larger group from which the study group has been drawn, and only when the research design does not include personal bias or systematic observational bias. Case studies are most appropriate for isolating critical independent or dependent variables. In many cases, the latter are then tested through experimental studies.

Experimental studies propose to establish a relationship between some independent variable (a variable—e.g., characteristic, behavior, procedure, curriculum, etc.—to be introduced into a group of subjects) and some dependent variable (a variable already present in the group). Despite the scientific rigor associated with experimental methods, pitfalls do exist. For example, the relationship between the variables is valid only under particular conditions. The presence of too many other independent variables may decrease correlation to the extent that ensuing predictions are no more accurate than mere chance. Furthermore, correlations rarely help determine cause and effect. Experimental research involves development of instruments that measure changes in behavior, selection of subjects, random assignment of the subjects to the treatment groups (control and experimental), introduction of the independent variable into the experimental group, posttesting, and analysis of results.

In recent years, a comparatively new experimental technique known as single-subject design has gained favor, particularly in the areas of contingency management and behavior modification. This design involves using small numbers of individuals to represent entire groups during the control and experimental phases of a study. It allows easy replication of the experiment, which is difficult and costly to accomplish for large groups.

E.   The Dynamic Process Underlying Project Design

1.   Laying the Foundation for a Collaborative Effort

Regardless of the level of anticipated collaboration by partner organizations, representatives from campuses within the school district or branches comprising a public library system, in addition to officials from partner organizations, should be included in the planning and conceptual design meetings. However, the mere presence of these individuals does not guarantee the cohesiveness needed to develop a winning proposal. Though the grantseeking team may consider themselves and the invited representatives a cohesive group united by a common purpose, careful negotiations are necessary to ensure that participants transcend their separate perspectives and begin to work in unison toward a shared goal.

The grant development team is responsible for developing a conceptual design for the project. Through a series of meetings, participants should prepare a statement describing the problem to be addressed, along with proposed enhancements, system reform, and restructuring of current programs and services. Representatives from each participating site, partner institution, parent organization, and key community group (as well as the library/automation sector, if applicable) should participate in the project discussions. Suggestions and other forms of input (e.g., excerpts of previous research) from each constituency must be incorporated into the project design to ensure success and continuation following the depletion of grant funds.

2.   Program of Action in Preparing the Team for Project Design

In preparing members of the grant development team for their tasks, a number of activities may be conducted. Each of these activities is a strategy for exploring potential changes. The team should participate in the activities that are new or appealing to them. If any team members are unwilling to participate in the activities, the group may elect to replace these individuals. These activities, designed to prepare the team as a whole and varying according to the experiences and expertise of the individuals involved, might include the following:

- Discussions among colleagues
- Visits to "best practices" sites
- Acquisition of research-based knowledge
- Professional development
- Preservice development
- Project support
- Technology initiative activities

Discussions Among Colleagues

The project design phase often begins with discussions among colleagues. Professional experiences (most notably, successful grant projects) of colleagues in sister institutions can provide team members with many valuable insights. In some cases, elements of another project might be incorporated into the team's design. Given the limited amount of time available to the grant development team, the replication of other models is sensible.

In the past, geographic considerations often precluded the option of a site visit to learn about other projects. Today, however, the Internet plays a role as a viable communications and learning tool; borrowing from colleagues has become considerably more efficient.

Visits to "Best Practices" Sites

For DOE guidelines for exemplary projects, see the following: 1. Mathematics, Science, and Technology Education Programs That Work: A Collection of Exemplary Educational Programs and Practices in the National Diffusion Network. Office of Educational Research and Improvement (ED), Washington, DC. Programs for the Improvement of Practice. 1994. 2. *Profiles of the Regional Educational Laboratories.* This handbook describes each laboratory's mission; key initiatives and ongoing work; "signature programs" developed by each lab; a few examples of recent, high quality publications and products from each lab; and information on how to contact each laboratory and the OERI program officer for that laboratory. Available at: http://www.ed.gov/prog_info/Labs. 3. ED402800 95 Benchmarking in Higher Education: Adapting Best Practices to Improve Quality. ERIC Digest. Author: Alstete, Jeffrey W. ERIC Clearinghouse. Available at: http://www.ed.gov/databases/ERIC_Digests/ed402800.html - size 12.3K.

Despite possible time and funding limitations, having team members visit a site that demonstrates "best practices" for exemplary projects may be appropriate. The directors of exemplary projects generally are accustomed to scheduling visits and working with planners interested in replicating their efforts. Whether or not the team decides to pursue such a visit, they should acquire the publications and related documentation available from exemplary projects, even if acquiring them requires a modicum of funding.

If the site is located within driving distance, the majority of team members may be able to participate in the visit. One of the participants should videotape the visit to share as much of the experience as possible with team members who do not attend. If the site is too remote, explore the possibility of arranging a videoconference. Although videoconferences are most easily arranged when the team has internal access to the necessary facilities (or access through partner organizations), inquiries should also be directed to universities and commercial studios.

Video transmission and travel to the conference site can be just as expensive as an actual visit. A detailed budgetary comparison will be necessary to determine which option is more cost effective.

Acquisition of Research-Based Knowledge

The research literature typically offers the most thorough means of examining successful operational models and accessing training and technical assistance from nationally recognized experts. A review of grant publications and reports is also necessary when determining how the proposed project might build upon prior projects.

Professional Development

For the DOE professional development guidelines (ED347493 Dec 92 The National Career Development Guidelines. ERIC Digest. Author: Miller, Juliet V. ERIC Clearinghouse on Counseling and Personnel Services, Ann Arbor, Mich., see the website at: http://www.ed.gov/databases/ERIC_Digests/ed347493.html - size 12.1K.

Professional development as a framework allows project participants to work with colleagues, regional experts, and acknowledged leaders in a given field. A series of focused learning experiences facilitates efforts by the grantseeking organization to build a staff who are better able to deliver projects and services to the target group.

Some grant development teams may consider it sufficient to have members prepare a list of topics for workshops and then merely carry through with the scheduled presentations. However, the more effective professional development frameworks combine a number of formal and informal educational formats, including workshops, seminars, site visits, teleconferences, formal graduate courses, instruction through the Internet, and independent study.

Engaging in one or more of these opportunities enables each team member to learn new methodologies and assessment techniques, identify strengths and weaknesses of models, and integrate the potentially valuable concepts into local projects and services. The primary goal is to find creative ways of implementing the components that will ensure success of the proposed project.

During the planning of professional development offerings, team members will

- plan and implement academic, instructional, and professional development activities and strategies to improve projects and services for the target group;

- identify ongoing continuing education opportunities that provide professionals with the knowledge and skills they need to maintain high standards of performance;

- determine ways of meeting the training needs of both administrators and support staff.

Professional Development in Public School Districts

Professional development activities in primary and secondary schools should focus on imparting to educators the knowledge and skills that will prepare them to help their students achieve academically. Increasing cultural diversity and continued technological developments are two major issues that grant development teams will have to contend with in future projects.

Professional Development in Public Libraries

With the twenty-first century rapidly approaching, information is universally recognized as a valuable commodity, and equitable access for all citizens is a mandate for public librarians. Geographic location, computing power, and telecommunications networks no longer dictate which information seekers will have access to needed data and which will not. The availability of professional development opportunities sponsored by consortia, societies, community-based organizations, institutions of higher education, and state government agencies will allow public librarians to keep abreast of the challenges posed by the rapid growth of information-intensive technologies.

Preservice Development

Designed specifically to meet the needs of future professionals who are fulfilling their last year of formal education, preservice development serves as a practice-based companion activity to theoretical classroom experiences. During the grant development process, the team may want to consider collaborating with an institution of higher learning that offers professional degrees in the appropriate fields. The deans of such programs might be contacted about establishing a preservice component related to proposal development. Academic officials approached in this manner are likely to perceive the advantages of providing to their students a work-environment opportunity that falls outside the realm of university expertise.

Project Support

Cultivation of ties with sister institutions, regional consortiums, state agencies, and other key organizations can provide a number of benefits:

- Access to resources unavailable internally
- The long-term development of cooperative relationships with other organizations.
- Greater responsiveness to community needs
- Greater likelihood of receiving letters of support for the project

As partner organizations become more intimately involved with the project, they generally will become more effective at providing needed support.

Technology Initiative Activities

Educators and librarians must comprehend both the potential and limitations of technology. In the development of alternative instructional models appropriate for the learning styles of an increasingly diverse user population, success is more likely to occur when the organization's technology experts plan thoroughly, install and maintain equipment properly, schedule and distribute use appropriately, and upgrade resources systematically.

Of even greater importance, however, educators and librarians must embrace technology. Administrators can play a key role by encouraging staff to master technology-based skills through self-instruction, formal education, workshops, and other types of training. Continuing education can be facilitated by developing instructional programs that are flexible enough to adapt to ever evolving uses and requirements. Educators and librarians need time to learn and experiment with new resources, identify useful components, and conceptually integrate them with existing materials.

F. Project Management

Setting policy and other administrative responsibilities falls within the jurisdiction of the applicant organization's governing body. Successful grantseekers tend to have a history of facilitating the involvement of everyone who has contributed something to a particular project. When a project involves the joint efforts of several organizations, governance functions most effectively through a collaborative group enfranchised to provide leadership and advise the applicant organization's administration.

To avoid a situation in which a single organization controls a collaborative project, the grant development team should design the governance structure. Although a collaborative project-governance structure has an advisory relationship to the applicant organization's administration, its presence—combined with the active participation of each partner organization—spreads project implementation among the major stakeholders.

1. Establishment of a Project Advisory Group

Encourage the chief administrator of each participating organization to select an official representative to serve in an advisory capacity to the project. Identify this body of representatives as an important constituent of the project. It is typically referred to by one of the following names: planning panel, advisory committee, or cooperating institutions council.

The body should include the following representation: the president of the applicant organization's governing body (or designated substitute), the chief administrator (or suitable replacement), one professional from each project site (selected by their peers), one parent or community member from each site (selected by the appropriate constituency group), representatives of advocacy groups (selected by their governing bodies), site administrators, business representatives (self-selected volunteers), a faculty member from each participating institution of higher education, and a representative from participating consortia. Membership in the group should also reflect the diversity of the community with regard to race, language, gender, disability, and socioeconomic characteristics.

Encourage all members to attend and contribute ideas to regularly scheduled meetings. By means of a formal set of session minutes, each participating organization should assist in gathering descriptive and empirical data, identifying models that may be available for replication, and considering recommendations for project implementation.

2.   Training for Advisory Group Members

The grant development team is more likely to enjoy a close working relationship with the advisory group if it designs a seminar to guide the representatives through the comprehensive planning process. Specific training topics should include the identification of needs; the development of vision, a mission statement, project goals, and project objectives; the identification of initiatives and activities to meet client needs; and evaluation strategies.

3.   Project Management in Public School Districts

Encourage educators to solicit campus improvement plans from mentor schools, "blue ribbon" sites, and other exemplary institutions throughout the United States. Based on site visits and documents delineating "best practices," the advisory body should review local campus improvement plans to determine components in need of revision.

Each of the components may be referred to as a Working Group of the advisory body. Upon selecting its own chairperson, the Working Group should coordinate its activities with all classroom teachers responsible for the component. In addition, the advisory body may decide to sponsor one or more public meetings to discuss the components with parents, business representatives, and other members of the community. It may also be worthwhile to incorporate into the revision process a suitable period for public feedback. Announcements for meetings and comment periods can be made through the school district's official newspapers, the mass media, and fliers distributed to students for home delivery.

When the members of each Working Group reach consensus, they should forward their revisions to the advisory body. The advisory body will incorporate revisions from all Working Groups into the revised campus improvement plan. Finally, the advisory body will submit the revised plan to the district administrators for adoption, and recommend it to the board of trustees for study and adoption.

The revised campus improvement plans should include strategies to

- ensure that all students have a fair opportunity to learn;

- improve teaching and learning;

- describe governance and management;

- strengthen parental and community involvement;

- expand improvements throughout the district.

Plans should also

- promote flexibility of campuses in developing plans that address the particular needs of their school and community that are consistent with the local improvement plans;

- outline a process of broad-based community participation in the development, implementation, and evaluation of the local improvement plan;

- describe how the district will encourage and assist schools in developing and implementing comprehensive school improvement plans;

- enumerate the strategies that the district can use to implement specific programs aimed at improving school readiness and improving the ability of students to learn effectively at all grade levels, by identifying the most pressing needs facing students and their families;

- identify any state and federal requirements that impede educational improvement.

4.   Project Management in Public Libraries

As with the school sector, public library administrators and trustees should be encouraged to solicit plans of services and programs from exemplary systems throughout the United States. Based upon site visits and documents delineating institutions involved in the delivery of quality services (including the Internet), the grant development team and library administrators should review local programming plans to determine components that merit revision.

A Working Group should then be established to facilitate the examination of each component. That body will coordinate its activities with branch managers and librarians responsible for the implementation process. The project personnel may choose to sponsor public meetings to discuss the components with patrons, business leaders, and other community representatives. A process for public input should be incorporated into the revision phase.

Once Working Group members reach consensus, they should forward their revisions to the advisory body. The advisory body will incorporate revisions from all Working Groups into the revised plan of services and programs. Finally, the advisory body will submit the revised plan to library administrators for consideration, and recommend it to the trustees for study and adoption.

The revised plan of services and programs should include strategies to

- ensure equity of access for all residents within the service area;

- improve services and programs available to the public;

- strengthen parental and community involvement;

- expand improvements throughout the public library system.

Such plans should also

- promote flexibility of branch libraries to develop plans that address the particular needs of their neighborhood that are consistent with the library system plan;

- describe a process of broad-based community participation in the development, implementation, and evaluation of the local improvement plan;

- outline the manner in which the public library system encourages individual branch libraries to develop and implement comprehensive plans of services and programs;

- enumerate the strategies that the library system and branches can use to implement specific programs aimed at improving access for all residents to print, multimedia, and Internet resources;

- identify any state and federal requirements that impede educational improvement.

G.   Parental Involvement with the Project

In recent years, parental involvement has become a key component of proposal development for projects designed to serve young children and students. Schools have long recognized the importance of the family, as well as other non-academic influences (e.g., health, safety, self-esteem), as determinants of academic achievement.

American society is built upon the premise that children will enter schools "ready to learn" (see Educate America Act: Goals 2000; 2 #1). This implies that children require parents who nurture their educational and emotional growth (i.e., listen, read, and talk to them; play with them; and simply spend time with them). For their part, schools must assist parents in supervising the growth and development of their children, as well as in preparing for the entry of these children into the school system.

Schools and libraries have a mandate to develop innovative grant proposals that can provide the needed education and skills to parents involved in laying the foundation for the educational and emotional growth of their children. In addition to health care and other social services, the projects developed by grantseekers should focus on ways of establishing and maintaining true parental involvement in the ongoing educational experiences of their children.

3
Project Narrative

The project narrative is the portion of the proposal that describes 1) the applicant, 2) the problem to be addressed, 3) the proposed solution, 4) the target population to be served, and 5) the expected benefits. The process of constructing the project narrative may involve a considerable commitment of time and effort. Even if the proposal does not ultimately secure funding, proposal preparation is nevertheless a worthwhile endeavor. Team members have the opportunity to develop and clarify ideas, better understand the project as a whole, and garner support from other organizations.

Writing a successful proposal is not beyond the capabilities of most educators and library professionals. Success depends on effectively planning the proposal development process (see Chapter 1); properly researching funding agencies; focusing the proposal to fit the interests of the targeted funding agency; and assembling an effective proposal package. Grantseekers should be aware of the various types of proposals that can be employed, particularly when the funding agency designates a preference:

- The **letter of intent**, generally no more than two pages in length, is employed when the funder requests to review a concise outline of the project as a condition for possibly reviewing a more comprehensive proposal. To be effective, this document must identify how the proposed project matches the funder's interests.

- The **letter proposal**, typically several pages in length, incorporates descriptions of the project plan, the applicant, and the specific request. This is the format requested by most businesses and corporations.

- The **comprehensive proposal** is frequently requested by foundations and government funders. This format enables the applicant to present additional pertinent information about the project and its value to the target population.

No matter what the characteristics of the funder may be or what type of proposal the funder requests, the information required in the narrative varies only slightly. The writing process will be greatly facilitated by gathering the materials and data outlined in Table 3-1 as part of an ongoing process to capitalize on grant opportunities as they present themselves.

Table 3-1

Developing a File in Preparation for Proposal Writing

General Information

- Mission statement of the organization

- Documentation regarding the organization's goals, history, and accomplishments

- Geographic area and number of people served by the organization

- Copy of the organization's most recent IRS tax exemption 501(c)(3) determination letter and tax identification number

- Names and affiliations of the organization's governing board

- Documentation regarding the organization's most recent audited financial statement and current operating budget

- Compilation of present sources of restricted and unrestricted funds

- Specification of the organization's operational structure, including geographically dispersed departments

- (for public school districts) Maps illustrating location(s), including specification of administrative centers and campuses within the system

Specific Information (for Public School Districts)

- Demographic data (staff, students, etc.)

- Number of schools within the district and grades taught at each school

- Census data (including population of the area, per capita income, graduation rates, educational levels of adults in the community, etc.)

- Total K–12 enrollment; percentages and enrollments by grade level, program (preschool, special education, etc.), race, gender, and other relevant factors.

- Standardized reading and math test scores, by school and grade level

- Total number of teachers, administrative staff, and professional staff

- Numbers of teachers, by grade, subject, and school

- Level of training of teachers and administrators

- Race and gender percentages of staff

- Average years of staff experience

- Per pupil expenditure

- Percentages of funds (local, state, federal)

- Student/teacher ratio and average class size

- Copies of assurances forms (for civil rights, Title IX, handicapped, etc.)

- Awards and other recognition of individual schools and associated faculty

The information required in the project narrative is typically structured within a set framework (see section B).

Despite nearly universal agreement as to the components of a grant proposal, the grantseeker should always follow the funder's guidelines. Although the grant-seeker might be tempted to include in the proposal's appendices supplemental materials that the funder specifically requested not be sent, doing so might compromise the likelihood of securing funding. In addition, the grantseeker should comply with designated page limits and formatting requirements. For instance, federal government agencies state that applications exceeding a specified length will be deemed ineligible for funding and returned to the grantseeker.

The unfortunate experience of one proposal development team illustrates the consequences of disregarding funder guidelines. The team's efforts encompassed four local education agencies collaborating over a three-month period to prepare a Title VII (Bilingual Education) grant proposal. Despite the input of many highly skilled personnel during the writing and documentation stages, a support staff member was delegated the key task of assembling the final document, copying it, packaging it, and sending it to the U.S. Department of Education immediately prior to the submission deadline. After the proposal had been submitted, team members began work on other assignments, confident that the project would receive a favorable review from the agency. When the project director received a letter from the funder two months later indicating that the appendices had exceeded the specified limit and, therefore, the entire five-year project had been disqualified, team members were devastated.

Vital to producing a coherent narrative is adherence to a well-planned drafting timetable. Each draft of the proposal should play a role in the ongoing conceptual design of the project. By keeping copies of all drafts generated during the writing process, team members establish a frame of reference, as well as a record of the changes that produced the final ideas and wording. The final draft will represent a collaborative effort built upon the insights of participants carefully selected for their capabilities (see Chapter 4).

The drafting stage will be more efficient if the various components of the proposal are first developed in outline form. The outlining process, in turn, will be more efficient if the functions of a proposal are first considered.

A.   Proposal Functions

A proposal serves five distinct functions, all of which are vital to the grantseeking process:

1. **Sales Piece.** In this respect, the proposal attempts to build a link between the applicant organization, its collaborating partners, and the funder. The narrative is concerned with "selling" a direct relationship between the funder's stated interests and the proposed project. The proposal development team must describe the project as a means of fulfilling the funder's interests. Effective articulation of this relationship increases the chances of securing funding.

2. **Concept Paper.** Delineation of the proposed project in a focused concept statement underscores its importance. The broad perspective employed here must encompass descriptions of the problem, a proposed solution based upon sound research principles, the target population, and the evaluation process.

3. **Plan.** The proposal outlines the steps that the project staff will follow to implement and evaluate the project, leading to the anticipated solution.

4. **Agreement.** Because the proposal specifies exactly what will be accomplished with grant funds, many funders want it included as part of the project contract.

5. **Evaluation Design.** The proposal provides a framework for reliable measurement of project results. Evaluation design generally includes two types of measurement: summative, or product, evaluation—to assess project accomplishments; and formative, or process, evaluation—to assess project efficiency. (See Chapter 6.)

B. Components of the Proposal

Some funders may specify letter-of-intent and letter-proposal formats, which do not involve the use of complex categorical headings. Many funders, though, particularly foundations and government agencies, are likely to specify a comprehensive-proposal format. Typical components (sections) of the comprehensive proposal include the following:

- Cover Sheet
- Abstract
- Table of Contents
- Introduction
- Needs Statement
- Goals and Objectives
- Project Design
- Key Personnel
- Budget
- Evaluation Design and Research Implications
- Dissemination of Findings, Results, Products
- Plan for Future Spending
- Appendices

Examples of some of these components are included in the discussion below. For more information about goals and objectives and project design, see Chapter 2; for more information about the budget, see Chapter 5; for more information about project evaluation, see Chapter 6.

1. Cover Sheet

The first page of the proposal document, the cover sheet is typically a standardized form identifying the project, funding agency, requested level of support, project title, submission date, and the applicant.

Reviewers generally read the title of a proposal first. The following suggestions should be considered when naming the proposal:

- Describe the project and its goal.
- Describe client or societal benefits.
- Be cautious in using acronyms.
- The title should be concise and easy to remember.
- Avoid "cute" titles.

Read the title to someone who knows little or nothing about the proposal, and then ask, "What do you think this proposal is about?" If the person is confused or uncertain, the title should likely be changed.

2.   Abstract

The abstract summarizes the proposal, typically including the following elements: need, goal, objectives, target population, procedures, evaluation, dissemination, and budget request total. It generally is 250 to 500 words (approximately one to two pages) in length. Ultimately, though, funder guidelines should dictate the length and content of the abstract.

Even though the abstract appears at the beginning of a proposal, it should be written last. Completing all other proposal components first will help clarify what should be summarized.

In some cases, the abstract is the only section read by the reviewer when screening proposals. Therefore, to motivate the reviewer to read the proposal, the abstract must be interesting and succinct.

3.   Table of Contents

All section titles and major headings of the proposal, along with corresponding pagination, should be included (verbatim) in the table of contents.

4.   Introduction

This section provides an opportunity to win (or lose) the reviewer's attention. An engaging opening line is essential. It might be an authoritative quotation from a historical figure, or an unsettling statement from, or about, a student in need. The following proposal excerpt is part of an introduction that successfully captures the reader's attention:

> Jennifer, an 11th grade student at Robert F. Kennedy High School, is worried—about whether she will be a good mother, about how she will support herself and her one-year-old baby, about locating and paying for child care and getting the baby there, about being able to participate in senior activities next year, and about finishing high school with her class.

Once the reviewer has been hooked, the introduction must "sell" the credibility of the grantseeking organization. Accordingly, it should communicate that the organization is fiscally secure, is efficiently managed, provides valuable services to its target groups, and has the respect of the community at large.

More specifically, the introduction should accomplish most, if not all, of the following:

- Clearly establish who is applying; when and how the organization was founded; and notable events in the organization's history.

- Describe the organization's philosophy, purposes, and goals.

- Outline the organization's programs, including its accomplishments and overall effect.

- Describe clients and constituents.

- Provide evidence of accomplishments, and endorsements or statements to establish the organization's overall credibility (e.g., staff qualifications, collaborative endeavors with other organizations).

- Establish credibility of the proposed project.

- Provide general information about the proposed project.

- Provide a transition to the needs statement.

Generally, this section should be written after completion of the project planning phase. In doing so, the grantseeker is more likely to succeed in conveying the importance of the project and the organization's qualifications to conduct it. Experienced grantseekers recommend that the introduction include an explanation of the organization's genesis, particularly the forces responsible for its growth and success; a concise discussion of its mission statement; and information about its current activities. Statistics and other relevant data can help convey a clear picture of the organization and the project's target population.

Many grantseekers use a template for the introduction. Minor modifications should be considered, however, to focus on factors of interest to the particular funding agency.

5. Needs Statement

The needs statement should explicitly indicate to the funder that a compelling problem or need exists and must be addressed. It should be written from the client's point of view, expressing a client need as opposed to a need of the organization. However, the needs statement should relate to the purposes and goals of the organization, and should be compatible with the organization's size and scope.

The needs statement must be supported by evidence drawn from a number of sources, including the organization's experiences and the testimony of appropriate experts. Also support the needs statement with research, including pertinent articles, studies, quotations, and statistics. Include statements from students, parents, teachers, and authorities on the project in question. Results of skills tests, report card grades, records of the number of economically disadvantaged students, and mobility rate for the school system provide effective documentation.

The scope of the needs statement should be realistic. Avoid trying to address every single need or problem of the organization. Discuss only those needs that can be met through the proposed project. Do not exaggerate a perspective of "doom and gloom" (i.e., the hopelessness of a given situation) and avoid stating possible solutions to a problem as the problem itself.

Mim Carlson, in her work, *Winning Grants Step by Step,* has set forth guidelines that embrace the chief concerns in producing an effective needs statement. They include:

- stating the need through the use of hard-core statistics rather than assumptions or undocumented assertions parading as facts;

- using statistics that are easily understood and that support your argument;

- using comparative statistics and research whenever possible;

- making sure all data collection is well documented;

- using touching stories of people as examples; and

- focusing your explanation of the need on the geographic area you are able to serve.

The following proposal excerpt successfully incorporates the key elements of a needs statement:

Increasingly, students face numerous barriers which impede academic progress and significantly reduce the likelihood of completing a high school education. In the United States, the number of students completing high school declined . . . At present, the state of Texas ranks . . . According to a recent report presented to the Appleton [Independent School District] Board of Trustees following an extensive dropout recovery program, Kennedy High School had a dropout rate of 10%. Eight of the 25 students with confirmed pregnancies, or 32%, dropped out of school before receiving a high school diploma, 22% higher than the rate of the total school population.

6.   Goals and Objectives

Project goals and objectives should proceed naturally from the needs statement. A project goal is a statement of the overall intent and outcome of the proposed project. It should relate directly to the purpose and priorities of the funding agency. A grant project should have only one or two goals.

Project objectives provide elaboration of the project goal by dividing it into a series of desired outcomes. Project objectives should be specific and measurable. They can include quantitative measures of accomplishment and qualitative descriptions of progress. Each objective should specify important factors of the action involved, such as what it will be, who will do it, whom it will affect, when it will be done, how it will be done, and at what level of accomplishment.

Project objectives can be further divided into process objectives and outcome objectives. Process objectives describe the methods employed to achieve the desired result. Outcome objectives describe the results.

Mim Carlson has provided examples of the goals and objectives that might be used for a particular social services program:

Goal
- The homebound elderly in ABC County will live with dignity and independence in their own homes.

Process Objectives
- Increase social services referrals and follow-up for 75 percent of the individuals served by the Meals Consortium during 1994–1995.

- Increase social services direct care to 90 percent of the most vulnerable homebound elders served by the Meals Consortium.

Outcome Objectives
- Reduce by five percent the number of individuals leaving the Meals Consortium to be institutionalized because of lack of social services.

- Expand care of the frail elderly to ensure that 80 percent of the population served by the Meal Consortium remain in their homes during 1994–95.

The following guidelines should be considered when writing project objectives:

- Address the outcomes of proposed activities.

- Avoid confusing the objectives with the activities themselves.

- Define the population to be served.

- Use numerical descriptions when possible.

- Use verbs such as *increase*, *decrease*, and *reduce*.

- Propose an achievable level of change in a specific period of time.

7. Project Design

Often referred to as the plan of action, the project design is typically the lengthiest section of the proposal. It specifies the activities and methods that will be used to achieve the project objectives (thereby achieving the project goal). It proceeds naturally from the project objectives, explaining what will be done, and how and when, to achieve them.

The project design describes a realistic sequence of activities and a timeline for achieving them. It explains why the activities were selected, and describes the methods, staff, and resources that will be used to achieve the activities. Charts, graphs, and tables can enhance the plan of action.

The following proposal excerpt shows how a project design might be worded:

The Pregnancy Related Services Program at Lennon High School will include the following project components and their measurable objectives:

1. Instruction in Skills and Knowledge for Parenting

    Objective: Each student will be instructed in essential elements. . . .

    Activities: Experts on teen pregnancy and parenting will present workshops. . . .

2. Job Readiness Training

    Objective: Each student will be provided job readiness training. . . .

    Activities: Texas Employment Commission eligibility workers will. . . .

3. Counseling

    Objective: The campus coordinator will serve students and provide counseling. . . .

    Activities: The campus coordinator will call students who do not return to school. . . .

4. Child Care

    Objective: Child care will be provided for students' children at licensed day care. . . .

    Activities: Students will be awarded day care slots on an as-needed basis.

5. Assistance in Obtaining Services from Government Agencies or Community Service Organizations

    Objective: Each student will be assessed for need and provided assistance. . . .

    Activities: The campus coordinator will assist students in accessing social services. . . .

8.   Budget

The budget delineates the costs and expenditures of conducting the proposed project. Most budgets have two components: the budget summary and the budget detail. The budget detail is developed first and typically itemizes costs under separate column headings: requested and donated (in-kind). The budget detail is usually divided into two categories: personnel and nonpersonnel. The personnel category includes wages and salaries, fringe benefits (e.g., FICA, health insurance) and sometimes consultant and contract services and travel expenses. The nonpersonnel category includes such items as equipment and supplies.

The budget summary, or narrative, is developed after compiling the budget detail. It provides a rationale for each budget item, which should relate to a project objective and activity, and summarizes the purpose of the request and how the cost was calculated. The intent of the budget summary is to relate the budget to the project design so that the budget presents no surprises to the reviewer.

Consider the following guidelines when writing the budget section of a proposal:

- Conduct research. Know exact prices for budget items.

- Check all math, twice. Errors can cause embarrassment and the perception of laziness or even dishonesty.

- Specifically describe budget items.

- Use only dollar amounts, never cents, in budget item totals. Round amounts when necessary.

9.   Evaluation Design and Research Implications

The evaluation process is primarily concerned with determining the effectiveness and efficiency of a project. Decisions made at this stage are vital in plotting the future direction of the project in addition to reassuring the funding agency that its investment is sound. More specifically, as noted by Mim Carlson, the evaluation process should be used to determine whether or not the project achieved its expected goal, to determine whether or not specified methods and objectives were used and achieved, to obtain feedback from the target group and others, to determine whether or not the identified need was met, to maintain control of the project, and to adjust the project during its operation to foster success.

The evaluation process assesses process and product. It includes evaluation of efficiency (formative evaluation), accomplishment (summative evaluation), and effectiveness (evaluation of overall worth and utility), using quantitative and qualitative methods. Evaluation may occur internally, externally, or both.

The evaluation design must identify who will monitor and evaluate the project, and must state the rationale used to select the evaluators. Evaluators are responsible for defining the evaluation criteria (indicators), describing the data collection methods and data analysis techniques, and communicating how the evaluation data will be directed toward project improvements.

The following guidelines should be considered when writing the evaluation design:

- Explain why evaluation is needed in the project.

- Define the meaning of *evaluation* as it relates to the project.

- Clearly identify the type and purpose of the evaluation and the audiences to be served by its results.

- Indicate that an appropriate evaluation procedure is included for every project objective.

- Provide a general organizational plan or model for the evaluation.

- Indicate why the scope of the evaluation is appropriate to the project. Illustrate the extent to which the project is practical, relevant, and generalized.

- Describe the information that will be needed to complete the evaluation, the potential sources of this information, and the instruments that will be used to collect it.

- Provide sufficient detail to indicate the technical soundness of all data collection instruments and procedures.

- Identify and justify procedures for data analysis, reporting, and use.

- Define standards that will be used in judging the results of the evaluation.

- Summarize any reports to be provided to the funding source based on the evaluation, and generally describe their content and timing.

- Identify any anticipated constraints on the evaluation.

The following proposal excerpt shows how an evaluation design might be worded:

> Students, parents, teachers, mentors and advisory committee members will participate in program evaluation, which will be both formative and summative, and which will include the following:
>
> - The number of students who access social services through the program
>
> - Attendance at family planning sessions
>
> - Student participation in the peer counseling program
>
> - Enrollment in vocational classes
>
> - Attendance at job readiness seminars

The scope of the project may preclude answering all the questions raised while conducting it. In such cases, the evaluator should assemble, categorize, and further elaborate upon the issues raised during the project. These activities will form the basis of any implications for further investigation to be addressed by other researchers.

10. Dissemination of Findings, Results, Products

Dissemination is the mechanism by which the grantseeker informs the funder and others about the project. The increasingly competitive nature of grantseeking requires an elaborate dissemination apparatus. In addition to informing others, dissemination will broaden support, locate more clients, alert others in relevant fields to new ideas, and add to the literature of the field in question.

Many dissemination strategies may be initiated in generic form and stored (e.g., in a vertical file, on diskette) prior to the final edit of the proposal. Dissemination options might include:

- Project newsletters circulated to selected individuals, influential decision makers, and organizations in the field

- Conferences and seminars (existing and new forums) hosted for individuals or groups likely to be interested in project results

- Site visits arranged for representatives of key professional associations

- Interim working papers describing project findings of immediate interest to other audiences

- Papers delivered at national conferences

- Articles prepared for scholarly, professional, or trade journals

- Pamphlets describing available project products and their potential uses

- Books or manuals issued by either the grantseeking organization, the funder, or commercial publishers

- Displays at appropriate meetings and conferences

- Demonstrations of techniques and presentations of materials developed by the project

- Agreements with other agencies to produce or market project results

- Audiovisual materials (e.g., films, slide shows, film strips, videotapes, television programs, etc.) produced internally or commercially

- Special briefings for key national or state officials

- Project staff appearances as speakers at local, state, and national meetings

- Press releases prepared for use by mass media

- Project documents filed with national information sources (e.g., National Technical Information Service)

- Model courses or seminars developed to show how the information resulting from the project can be explained to others in a formal instructional setting

- Training sessions to show individuals in other organizations how to conduct in-service workshops or provide consulting services for practitioners interested in project materials

- Self-instructional modules developed to train others to use project results (without requiring attendance at formal training sessions)

- Project findings disseminated through computer networks (e.g., BITNET, Internet)

- Key reports or outcomes stored on diskette (or recordable compact disks) for exchange among personal computer users

- Executive summaries of project results faxed to appropriate persons

The proposal should include those dissemination options that are most likely to further the objective of informing those individuals and agencies who would be interested in the project. While the grantseeker can afford to be selective in choosing from among the wide array of options, a sufficient number should be included to ensure optimum publicity for the project.

11.   Plan for Future Spending

The funder, committed to the continued life of the project, often requires a description of precisely how project funding will continue after the grant expires. By outlining a plan for continuation, the applicant demonstrates commitment and support for the project while emphasizing an obligation to continue the project. The funder is likely to be interested in plans that address the prospect that support might have to be obtained from other sources.

Sources for continuance funds include the following:

- other funders (government, corporate, private)

- membership fees

- service fees

- user charges

- wealthy individuals/philanthropists

- product sales

- publications

- direct mail

- bequests

- memorial gifts

- telethons

- capital campaigns

Many of these sources may not prove viable for the grantseeker. The following questions can assist in identifying the best sources for potential continuance funds:

- Can the organization absorb future funding responsibilities within its general operating budget within the next few years?

- Can the project be supported by service fees?

- Can a third party be contracted to subsidize services to clients?

- Can the organization raise nongrant funds to support future expenses?

- Can another profitable service or activity be expanded to support future funding of the project?

- Can the financial responsibility for continuing the project be transferred to another organization?

12. Appendices

Although proposal reviewers do not always carefully read the appendices, this section could help secure funding when the proposal is compared with others. Appendices include attachments that expand concepts presented in the proposal and present information peripheral to the proposal. In the project narrative, each appendix item should be referred to by page number. Appendices typically include:

- Mission statement of the organization

- Vitae of project director, other key personnel, consultants

- List of board members and officers with titles

- List of advisory committee members

- List of other organizations providing funding

- Verification of nonprofit status; IRS certification

- Bibliography

- Curriculum listings

- Studies/research, including tables, graphs, charts

- Letters of commitment, endorsement

- Newspaper or magazine articles and pictures favorably mentioning the organization

- Maps

- Certifications

- Provisions and assurances

- Audited financial statement

- Definitions of terms

- Subcontract data

- Consortia agreements

- Tabular data

- Recent annual reports, fiscal reports

- Past-success stories, noteworthy case histories

- Agency publications

- Publicity

C.   Cover Letter

Although not a part of the proposal proper, the cover letter is an essential attachment. It serves primarily to reintroduce the applicant to the funder. In some cases, it may be useful to refer to a prior communication between the applicant and a particular member of the funder's staff, and note any modifications to the proposal prompted by this communication.

According to David Bauer, author of *The Complete Grants Sourcebook for Higher Education* (Third Edition, 1995), the cover letter should be brief (approximately half a page), should motivate the reader to want to see the entire proposal, should indicate dramatic need or uniqueness, and should state the grantseeker's case in unique fashion. In addition, the applicant may use the cover letter to emphasize organizational commitment. It may be worthwhile to have the organization's board president and chief administrator both sign the letter (including more than one signature is an acceptable practice).

D.   Proposal Writing, Design, and Organization Guidelines

Consider the following guidelines when writing the narrative:

- Study and imitate good writers. Perhaps the best preparation for the writing process is reading and critiquing other proposals. Whenever possible, interact with writers widely acknowledged by their peers to be among the best at their trade.

- Use action verbs throughout the text.

- Vary sentence structure.

- Avoid excessive or unnecessary use of commas. Commas slow reading. Excessive use of commas can indicate overly complicated sentences, or sentences that contain too much information.

- Use short, succinct paragraphs.

- Write to communicate, not to impress. Avoid abstract, verbose, and decorative language; use concrete, simple words. Avoid overuse of acronyms, "educationese," jargon, and buzzwords. Terms commonly employed within one's profession may be incomprehensible—or even offensive—to potential funders.

- Avoid tentative and "hopeful" statements; they do not inspire confidence. Use definitive statements (e.g., use *can* and *will* rather than *may* and *might*).

- Document statements when necessary. Avoid unsupported assumptions.

- Use lists to indicate steps in a sequence, materials or parts needed, items to remember, criteria for evaluation, conclusions, and recommendations.

- Check spelling. If using the spell checker feature of word processing software, remember that it cannot identify misused words. Proofread, and have a colleague repeat the process.

- Above all, follow the funder's instructions precisely.

To ensure that the writing is easily understood and unlikely to distract the reader, have an individual outside the organization proofread the proposal. Emphasize the importance of clarifying any vagueness that might exist within the narrative.

Consider the following guidelines when designing the proposal:

- Use simple, unadorned fonts, and a minimum of different fonts.

- Use bullets to reinforce the message without being wordy.

- Use bold-face type, rather than underlined or italic type, for emphasis.

- Use liberal margins and spacing. The left and right margins should be wide enough (at least one inch) to allow for thumbspace (i.e., it should be possible to hold each page of the proposal without the thumbs covering the type). Use ragged right margins, which are easier to read than right-justified margins because the proportional spacing of justified text slows reading. Use white space to emphasize statements.

- Indent paragraphs five spaces to increase readability.

- Include charts and graphs in the narrative when absolutely essential to the emphasis of the proposal; otherwise, they belong in the appendices (as with all appendices, cross-references should be included at a relevant place within the text). Use simple bar, line, or pie charts and graphs; complicated displays will distract the reader.

- Use headings and subheadings, but no more than three levels (otherwise, the reader may become lost in the structural detail of the proposal). Level-one headings should be centered, bold-face type, all capital letters; triple space before beginning text. Level-two headings should be left-justified, bold-face type, proper nouns and other keywords capitalized; triple space before beginning text. Level-three headings should be indented, keywords capitalized, bold subheading, and separated with appropriate punctuation (e.g., period) before continuing with paragraph copy.

- Use color, graphics, and illustrations when appropriate. A reader generally notices illustrations before text, and large illustrations before small ones. Determine the size of the illustration using the "three-fifths rule": Page layout is more dramatic and appealing when the major element (illustration, blocks of text) occupies more than half of the available space.

- Use standard 8½-by-11-inch white paper, unless the funder indicates otherwise. Use 20-weight bond paper, a moderately high quality but reasonably priced paper that will photocopy or print well in laser printers. Always send the original document rather than a photocopy or fax, unless directed otherwise by the funder. Do not use brightly colored paper; it is distracting.

- Use staples rather than fancy bindings. Most funders request that the proposal be stapled in the upper left corner. If the document is too thick for a staple, substitute a "bulldog" clip.

Once the proposal has been completed, a checklist such as Table 3-2 should be used to ensure that all the vital information and necessary components are present.

Table 3-2

**A Checklist of Key Components for Submission
to Funding Source**

❑ Postcard. Stamped, self-addressed card for the funder to use to notify the applicant that the proposal arrived before the deadline

❑ Cover Letter. Reintroduces the applicant to the funder; provides information about the applicant, the organizational commitment, and the nature of the grant request

❑ Cover Sheet. Identifies the project, funding agency, requested level of support, project title, submission date, and the applicant

❑ Abstract. One- to two-page synopsis of the project

❑ Table of Contents. A list of all section titles and major headings, along with corresponding pagination

❑ Introduction. Background information about the applicant; establishes qualifications and credibility

❑ Needs Statement. Statement, documentation, and explanation of the problem to be addressed, expressed in terms of the target population

❑ Goals. Statements of the overall intents and outcomes of the proposed project, expressed as relevant to the funder's interests

❑ Objectives. Specific, measurable outcomes that will allow the project to achieve its goals

❑ Project Design. Description of the activities and methods that will be used to achieve project objectives, including a timeline, and management plan

❑ Key Personnel. Responsibilities and qualifications of individuals who will conduct the project, including the project director/principal investigator, staff, evaluator, and collaborators (often included in the project design)

(Table 3-2 continues on page 64.)

Table 3-2—Continued

☐   Budget. Summary and detail of project expenses, with justification for each item

☐   Evaluation Design. Identification of the evaluator, specification of evaluation criteria, and description of data collection methods and analysis techniques

☐   Dissemination. Plans for sharing results with others in the field

☐   Plan for Future Spending. Description of how project funding will continue after the grant expires; indicates the applicant's commitment to the project and obligation to continue the project

☐   Expected Outcomes. Explanation of anticipated project results as they relate to objectives. This section provides a bridge to future projects and/or research to be undertaken by other organizations.

☐   Appendices. Attachments that expand proposal concepts and present peripheral information (e.g., a statement of nondiscrimination)

4

Project Personnel

The grantseeking organization must convince the funder, through the grant proposal, that available personnel have the capabilities to 1) fulfill the major responsibilities of the project, 2) perform (or supervise those who perform) the activities promised in the application, 3) exercise proper stewardship of the funds, 4) comply with all legal requirements and all funder requirements, and 5) report all requested information to the funder in a timely and appropriate manner.

A. Project Staffing Requirements

In selecting key personnel for a proposed project, the grantseeking organization must consider the objectives to be accomplished, the time and organizational commitment required for project management and supervision, the number of individuals required to accomplish the objectives, and the responsibilities and time commitment required of each participant. The following questions should be asked:

- What qualifications does the project require of the project director and project coordinator?

- What qualifications does the project require of each of the other key personnel?

- Is experience an essential requirement for key personnel?

- How much time will each person commit to the project?

- How will the organization ensure that key personnel are selected without regard to race, creed, national origin, gender, age, economic status, or handicapping condition?

B.   Local Personnel Available to the Project

Whenever possible, project personnel should be selected from within the local organization. Key personnel should be individuals who

1.   possess a thorough knowledge of the organization and its employees and clients;

2.   are stakeholders in the organization and the successful implementation of its mission;

3.   understand the organization's current mission and future vision; and

4.   can articulate the organization goals clearly and convincingly.

Federal and state grant funding agencies usually provide funds for hiring new personnel for the projects they sponsor. In writing a proposal, a provision for salary continuation beyond the funding period must be included. Inexperienced grant-seekers sometimes make the mistake of cutting the personnel budget to increase funding available for purchase of materials and supplies. This error can result in the loss of points during the evaluation process because funding agencies frequently conclude that local personnel (particularly those designated for key positions) who already have full-time jobs will be unable to devote adequate time to the proposed project.

Similarly, designating a current employee as project director can place a proposed project at risk. Unless assured otherwise, the funder may assume that such a director cannot devote adequate time to this pursuit. Appointing (or hiring) an employee to relieve the project director of current routine tasks, thereby allowing more time for project-related activities, can provide such assurance.

C.   Functional Capabilities Statements for Key Project Personnel

1.   Project Director

The qualifications for managing the proposed project must be primary criteria when selecting the project director. This individual hires, trains, organizes, and supervises other project employees, and coordinates the project and its development. The director must be an effective leader—someone whose encouragement sparks other participants' awareness that their capabilities are necessary for the project's success.

The individual with the most experience and expertise relevant to the project is the logical choice for project director. For example, a project related to development of the automation infrastructure of a regional library consortium requires a director conversant not only in a broad framework of interlibrary cooperation but also cabling and other educational technologies. Because unexpected events and delays are likely to affect any project, the role of project director requires inherent flexibility. The project director leads other key personnel in making necessary adjustments.

The project director's responsibilities begin during the planning process and continue through and beyond the duration of the project. The following list is a sampling of typical responsibilities:

1. Ensure that the proposal includes adequate descriptions of all project components.

2. Review the funder's award notice and conditions; disseminate to all project personnel.

3. Establish and maintain contact with the funder.

4. Review and disseminate funder regulations that affect the project.

5. Review and disseminate to project participants the organizational policies and procedures for the grant development process.

6. Supervise execution of the project.

7. Hire and supervise project personnel, both internal and contracted.

8. Monitor and adhere to the project budget.

9. Check and maintain documentation of all budgeted expenditures.

10. Negotiate and coordinate budget amendments with the funder.

11. Maintain documentation of all budget amendments.

12. Document matching funds.

13. Submit, in a timely manner, formative progress reports, evaluations, and other forms required by the funder during the project period.

14. Monitor inventory of grant-funded equipment and supplies.

15. Submit an application for continuance funds.

16. Submit required reports and documentation to the funder.

Because the project director is largely responsible for the success of a project, information about the project director, including general background, educational degrees and unique educational experiences, and project management experiences, should be documented in the grant proposal.

When the proposal does not request funding for the project director's salary, the proposal should indicate the percentage of time the individual will devote to the project. The budget will indicate that percentage of the project director's salary as in-kind.

The following excerpt, from a funded proposal, describes an individual's qualifications to serve as project director:

> The executive director of elementary schools holds both bachelor's and master's degrees, as well as mid-management and professional supervisor's certifications. She is responsible for curriculum and instruction super-vision of all 25 elementary schools in the district. Since 1985, each time the district has built a new elementary or intermediate school, she has been responsible for determining the boundary lines and making sure the district is in compliance with the court-ordered desegregation plan. She will disseminate information from Central Office to the school campuses. The district will provide as in-kind the salary and benefits of the project director. She will devote approximately 30 percent of her time to this program.

2.   Other Personnel

The proposal should also document the extent to which other key personnel are qualified to fulfill project responsibilities. Documentation should include educational degrees, certifications, and experiences. The following proposal excerpt describes relevant qualifications of other key project personnel:

> Ten specialists currently serve the district as subject-area consultants. They report to the director of curriculum and instruction. All are certified in supervision. The consultants are responsible for providing technical assistance and subject-area expertise to the schools, keeping abreast of new developments in education, disseminating information to teachers and administrators, supervising the planning and implementation of curriculum, advising on the use of instructional materials, assisting with comprehensive planning, organizing and conducting staff development, supervising and monitoring scope and sequence for effective learning, and supervising and monitoring departmental budgets. The district will provide as in-kind the salaries and benefits of all consultants, who will devote approximately 15% of their time to the implementation of this project.

3.   Library Media Specialist

The role of school library media specialist has expanded and requires increased technological expertise to serve students' needs. The following position description assisted in securing a grant:

> The director of library media and computer technology, an educator for 27 years, earned a bachelor of arts in education degree and a master of library science degree. She has presented at numerous local and state conferences and has chaired several local and state committees and events. She is editor of the state newspaper for school librarians. She supervises school librarians on all 48 district campuses. In staffing the district libraries and in building collections, she and her colleagues seek to provide ethnic diversity and well-balanced, multicultural literature to complement the district's curriculum and its diverse student population.
>
> The director stays abreast of computer technology, and as supervisor of the district technology specialists, is directly involved with the computer instructional curriculum. She also oversees the purchase and implementation of computer hardware and software by staff and students. The district will provide as in-kind the director's salary. She will devote approximately 20% of her time to this program.

D.   Provisions and Assurances

1.   Hiring and Employment Compliances

Most federal and state grant applications include printed hiring and employment compliances in the "Provisions and Assurances" section, usually the last part of the application. It must be signed by the person who is authorized to legally bind the applicant in a contract. The section cites specific federal laws, rules, and regulations pertaining to the contract project, including the Americans with Disabilities Act, the Civil Rights Act of 1964, and the Age Discrimination Act of 1975. During the proposal evaluation process, no points are awarded if the signed assurances are included with the application, but failure to include them results in proposal disqualification.

The section of the grant proposal concerning key personnel should contain the organization's statement of nondiscrimination. The following proposal excerpt can serve as a model:

> This district does not discriminate against persons because of race, creed, national origin, age, sex, economic status or handicapping condition in employment, promotion or educational programming. Any employee, parent or student who has a complaint which cannot be resolved at the campus level through the principal may submit a complaint or grievance in writing to the superintendent of schools at . . . .

Proposal readers expect applications to go a step further than quoting their organization's nondiscrimination statement. Applicants should prove that their organization does not simply display an attractively framed document prominently on office walls by explaining the steps being taken to assure nondiscrimination for all, such as training new employees and providing ongoing training for all employees.

2. Government Compliances

The "Provisions and Assurances" section within most federal and state grant applications includes printed compliance statements that must be signed by the person who is authorized to legally bind the applicant in a contract. The section contains information about subcontractors, purchases of equipment and supplies, federal laws, rules and regulations that apply to the contract, record maintenance, and educational practices. It cites specific federal regulations that apply to federally funded applications submitted by local education agencies, education service centers, institutions of higher learning, nonprofit organizations, state agencies, and commercial (for-profit) organizations. Because signing these compliances obligates the applicant to comply with all provisions and assurances throughout the life of the project, they must be understood and observed precisely.

5
Budget Development

A. The Role of the Budget

The budget section of a proposal delineates the expenses for conducting a project. Budgeting does not require any exceptional aptitude for math or accounting. Rather, success is more directly related to the effort spent gathering and organizing necessary data.

The budgeting process for nonprofit organizations pursuing grant funds has become more complex in recent years. Funders have increased their demands regarding accountability for and justification of financial allotments. All funding agencies are likely to have idiosyncratic requirements and procedures; nevertheless, funding agencies expect compliance from applicants. Frequently, applicants are required to explain the expected outcomes associated with requested funds; in short, the projected results that will ensue from the expenditure of budgetary allotments.

B. Types of Budgets

There are a variety of budget types to choose from, each suited to particular purposes:

- formula budgets

- zero-based budgets

- lump-sum budgets

- line-item budgets

- performance (functional) budgets

- program budgets

Formula and zero-based budgets presume, respectively, a broad institutional environment and a continuity of overall service provision, both of which generally are outside the concerns of grant development.

A lump-sum budget refers to the complete amount budgeted at the top of an organization to specific departments, divisions, or locales. Each subgroup is responsible for further dividing the lump-sum allotment using one of the other budgetary techniques. Due primarily to the fact that the lump-sum budget does not readily lend itself to financial oversight, it is not typically used in grant proposals.

A line-item budget is the most universally employed type, particularly in meeting funding agency requirements for grant proposals. This budget is an itemization of expenditures by category. Project expenses generally are divided into two major categories: personnel costs and operating costs. Personnel costs are subdivided into salaries, fringe benefits, and so on; operating costs are subdivided into space usage, equipment, communications, copying, printing, travel, supplies, and so on.

Functional and program budgets offer a greater degree of sophistication and control than is possible by merely itemizing costs. They format budgetary data in a manner that allows more efficient management and allocation of resources. A functional budget groups together line-item costs for one particular function or activity. Employing this approach, the project team can ascertain the costs of performing specific functions or activities. A program budget focuses on the costs associated with the objectives of a particular project. In this manner, the project team can determine the cost differences between objectives and, by extension, the activities comprising each objective.

All these budget types are closely interrelated. The grant project probably represents a small part of the overall scheme of services provided by an organization. In this case, the line-item budget, as a whole, can be interpreted as both a functional and a program budget. Elements of functional and program budgets can be combined, as shown in Table 5-1.

C. Budget Preparation

Most organizations possess established guidelines for calculating budgetary expenditures. In larger organizations, these guidelines are likely to be explicitly detailed and rigorously followed. Experts within the accounting department will be available to advise the grant development team regarding the determination of specific expenses. Accountants can provide cost figures based upon information concerning a project's projected use of the organization's resources. For example, a school library's resources might include photocopying, communications (e.g., telephone, fax, etc.), utilities (e.g., air conditioning, heating, etc.), mail delivery, and maintenance. More established organizations are also likely to have cost figures readily available (e.g., employee salary ranges) to facilitate the budgeting process.

Smaller or less established organizations may lack specific guidelines for determining budgetary expenditures. In addition, they often cannot provide the services of an accountant. In such cases, budget development requires greater involvement from the grant development team. Table 5-2, pages 74-76, provides basic guidance for preparing a proposal budget when external assistance is minimal.

(Text continues on page 77.)

Table 5-1

Example Combined Functional and Program Budget

PROGRAM BUDGET

Functional Budget Activities	*Objective 1* Increase computer literacy among Staff	*Objective 2* Students
Develop Training Units		
Line Items		
Personnel	$20,000	$10,000
Equipment	$12,000	$9,750
Supplies/materials	$3,500	$2,500
Copying/binding	$1,000	$850
Facilities	$1,000	$750
Activity Subtotal	$37,500	$23,850
Conduct Staff Workshops		
Line Items		
Personnel	$30,000	$0
Equipment	$3,500	$0
Supplies/materials	$3,000	$0
Copying/binding	$1,000	$0
Facilities	$750	$0
Activity Subtotal	$38,250	$0
Conduct Student Labs and Classroom Sessions		
Line Items		
Personnel	$0	$12,500
Equipment	$0	$3,000
Supplies/materials	$0	$2,750
Copying/binding	$0	$750
Facilities	$0	$750
Activity Subtotal	$0	$19,750
Totals by Objective	$75,750	$43,600

Project Total: $119,350

Table 5-2

Proposal Budget Preparation

Personnel Expenses

Determining Qualifications

Consider staff qualifications needed to conduct the project by answering the following questions:

- Which staff must be professionally trained on the job (i.e., during the project)?

- Can student interns be used?

- What clerical staff are needed?

Determining Time Commitments

Determine the time commitment required by each position by considering the following information:

- Proposed timeline for the project

- Data from comparable projects (if available)

- Capabilities of available personnel

An understanding of relevant buzzwords is also necessary. The unit frequently used to quantify paid employee time is the "full-time equivalent" (FTE), which is expressed as a decimal. A 1.00 FTE indicates that the total amount of paid service is the equivalent of one person working full time for 12 months. Any FTE value less than 1.00 indicates the decimal proportion of a twelve-month full-time job for which the person will be or has been employed. Another common unit is "percent of time," which is expressed as a percentage. For example, 50% time (or .50 FTE) indicates a half-time position.

Determining Salaries

For each position, analyze the local marketplace (employment advertisements, salary distribution ranges available from private- and public-sector organizations, etc.) to determine salaries for comparable positions. After obtaining this data, consider special skills that may be required, as well as personal perceptions about fair reimbursement for the position.

Personnel Expenses Sample Budget

Personnel	FTE	Salary Range (monthly)	Budget Request
Executive director	.05	$4,000–5,000	$2,250
Project director	1.00	$3,500–4,500	$48,000
Library consultant	1.00	$2,500–3,500	$36,000
Clerical	.50	$1,250–1,750	$18,000
Subtotal Personnel Costs			$104,250
Employee benefits (20% of salary)			$20,850
Total Personnel Costs			$125,100

Some budgets will qualify the FTE, indicating that it is "subject to change over the contract year." This provides flexibility in the contract in case there is a vacancy in the position or some other need to deviate slightly from the stated time commitment.

At the minimum, employee benefits cover employer contributions to federal and state governments (e.g., taxes, unemployment insurance, social security contributions, etc.). This category may also include health and dental insurance and retirement funds.

Operating Expenses

Begin by analyzing the proposal to ascertain all the items that will require funding. Typical categories comprising operating expenses appear in the sample budget below. Many government funders have fixed reimbursement rates for items such as mileage, per diem, and consultants. Some expenses may be the grantseeker's responsibility (e.g., refreshments at training sessions).

Inexperienced grantseekers may want to contact the chief executive officer of an agency similar to that of the chosen funder for assistance in preparing this portion of the budget. Local educational service centers and university grants offices can typically supply the most current reimbursement rates, as can the state board of control that annually establishes the rates. The grantseeker should avoid contacting the funder for such information. An appearance of inexperience may affect the funder's confidence in the grant proposal.

(Table 5-2 continues on page 76.)

Table 5-2—Continued

Some budgetary allotments will likely be changed during the negotiation stage with the funder. For instance, the funder might request that a line-item request for the purchase of a computer workstation be changed to a leasing arrangement. Regardless, the grantseeker must precisely follow all funder instructions regarding preparation of the budget. Typically, funders state their instructions, including notable restrictions, within the grant application.

Operating Expenses Sample Budget

Operating Expense	Budget Request
Conferences	$1,000
Educational materials	$750
Equipment (rental and maintenance)	$5,000
Insurance (liability)	$4,000
Office supplies	$1,750
Online computer use	$2,500
Printing	$2,300
Rent (1,000 sq. ft. @ $1 per sq. ft. x 12 mos.)	$12,000
Telecommunications	$6,200
Utilities	$20,000
Total Operating Expenses	$55,500

Budget Justifications

For line-item budgets, some funding agencies will request more detailed descriptions of the items, including calculation explanations. Line items can be thoroughly described and explained using a method called budget justification. The following proposal excerpt is an example:

> Travel expenses: Primarily mileage, driving to and from school library sites and central computer facilities for an estimated 400 miles per month at 25 cents per mile (state-approved rate) times 12 months for a total of $1,200. Also included is $1,500 for transportation and per diem (at State Board of Control rates) to two conferences—one, national, and the other, international, in scope—to present the project findings. The total request for travel is $2,700.

D.   Additional Budgeting Considerations

1.   The Influence of Funding Agencies on Budget Formatting

Government agencies typically use specially prepared budget forms with extensive directions. Deviations from the explicit line-item breakdown they require—for example, the shifting of funds from one sector to another—are permissible only when the applicant organization has made a formal request for these changes. Private and corporate funders often allow a more generalized line-item format built around expense categories. This generalized approach permits more leeway in cost allocation; it is usually acceptable for the grant recipient to shift funds from one category to another without obtaining permission from the funder. Regardless of the format, applicants must precisely comply with all requirements set forth by the funding agency.

2.   Matching Funds and In-Kind Contributions

The act of assuming particular expenses by the applicant organization is considered an "in-kind" contribution to the proposed grant project. The funding agency may ask the grantseeker to supply matching funds comprising a specified portion of the total request. The funder may also require that the sources of matching funds be identified. Table 5-3 shows one method of documenting such sources, while Table 5-4 shows a specific in-kind personnel budget.

Table 5-3

Sources of Matching Funds Budget

Sources of match (check where applicable):   ❑ In-Kind   ❑ Cash

In-Kind Match Breakdown

Line Item	Total Value	Source of Match
Salaries	$25,000	Revenue sharing
Rent	$3,600	General fund
Equipment	$2,800	Corporate gift
Total	$31,400	

Cash Match Breakdown

Source: Amount:

Table 5-4

In-Kind Personnel Budget

Personnel	FTE	Funding Request	Agency In-Kind	Total
Superintendent	.10	$7,500	$0	$7,500
Project director	1.00	$35,000	$17,500	$52,500
Librarian	.50	$15,000	$0	$15,000
Auto. consultant	1.00	$40,000	$0	$40,000
Clerical	.50	$0	$10,000	$10,000
Total		$97,500	$27,500	$125,000

3. Budget Adjustments and Amendments

A budget adjustment is the transfer of funds from one category (line) to another. Funding agencies—particularly state and federal government entities—requiring a line-item budget generally do not permit the grant recipient to engage in this practice without making a formal request. When funds are transferred, the adjusted budget should clearly identify the lines where money has been either added to or subtracted from the original figure. In addition, a written explanation for the transfer should be attached.

When the scope of the project is significantly modified, the funder will often require the applicant to submit a budget amendment. Typically, this happens when the funding agency requests that another activity be added to the project, for which the applicant would be provided more money. Amendments generally are documented in the same manner as adjustments.

4. Contract Negotiations

Once a proposal has been approved, some funding agencies will insist on formal contract negotiations. This process may include discussion of one or more of the following:

- Decreasing/increasing the amount of requested funding

- Changing the wording of contract provisions

- Stating the rationale for the implementation activities

- Changing or adding goals, objectives, and activities

- Clarifying particular sections of the narrative

During negotiations, the grantseeker must understand how even minor changes could affect the project as a whole. Avoid conceding to funder demands simply to obtain the money and begin the project. If the funder wants to negotiate, a compromise can likely be achieved. Remember that the funder is equally committed to the success of the project.

One source provides the following recommendations for the negotiation process:

- Reread the proposal immediately before entering into negotiation. Make sure you are intimately familiar with all of its provisions.

- Create an atmosphere of partnership with the contract negotiator.

- Proceed cautiously when considering changes. Look at the impact any change will have on other objectives.

- Be prepared to discuss your reasons for keeping the project as initially developed in the proposal.

- If the agency has not been awarded the full amount requested, prepare a new version of the proposal in advance of the meeting. This enables you to have time to rethink the budget and program, and decide what revisions you are willing to make.

- Remember to "maintain your integrity." If you know that the agency cannot do the job for the amount of money offered, despite changes to make it most cost-effective or negotiations with the funder to reshape the project, the agency will need to decide if it is worth pursuing. It is possible that the agency will choose to turn down the contract because accepting it would prove too costly.

5.   Subcontracts

Subcontracting involves formally arranging within the grant proposal for another organization to provide a particular service. The subcontractor is required to abide by the same contractual terms as the primary contractor. The primary contractor, though, is responsible for ensuring that the subcontractor fulfills these terms; this is usually accomplished by means of an additional contract. To establish credibility, the applicant must clearly specify in the grant proposal the role of the subcontractor.

6
Project Evaluation

A. Overview of the Evaluation Process

An evaluation process—the guarantee of accountability for measured project results—must be built into every proposal. An evaluation design explains how the effectiveness of the proposed project will be assessed. It includes detailed descriptions of the criteria, or evidence, that will be collected with regard to each project objective; and the instruments and methods that will be used to collect this data. The evaluation must produce the comparative information necessary to judge project accomplishments against stated objectives.

While the evaluation design must clearly state the criteria for success, it should also include a plan for modifying methods and activities during the course of the project. It should state when, and from whom, evaluation data will be collected. Evaluation reports are another vital component of the process; the design should clearly state how and when evaluators will report their findings to the funder.

Though the primary purpose of evaluation is to assess project accomplishments, a good evaluation will assess project efficiency as well. Formative evaluation is used to assess project efficiency, while summative evaluation is used to assess project accomplishments.

Evaluators should be determined during the planning stage of the grant proposal process. The grantseeker should consider whether or not external evaluators (outside the organization) will be used and, if so, begin contacting potential candidates.

B.   Evaluation Methods

1.   Formative Evaluation

A formative evaluation measures the efficiency of the project process. The evaluator accomplishes this by assessing implementation of the project at various times throughout the project year, reporting results that identify necessary adjustments and improvements. Project procedures are then modified to achieve stated objectives.

The following proposal excerpt is from a formative evaluation design:

> The assessment of the implementation of this project will be conducted by a three-member team of impartial educators from outside the district. The evaluator, an independent consultant, will serve as head of the team. The team will also include two experienced administrators who have run successful grant-funded programs.
>
> The team will visit each school, for at least a day at a time, three times during the school year. The evaluator will obtain qualitative and quantitative data through classroom observations; records analysis; interviews with parents, teachers, and students; and through a survey of teachers and students. The information will be used to
>
> - identify problems encountered in program implementation, thereby noting situations that need immediate attention and may explain project outcomes;
>
> - generate recommendations that may be useful in making necessary changes to improve the program;
>
> - determine the adequacy of program services for the entire range of students;
>
> - provide information that will be useful in informing the public about the progress of the program.
>
> The assessment team will provide both an oral and a written report. These reports will be given to the principals of the schools, and the evaluator will be available to meet with the school faculty. The team will meet with the Advisory Committee and provide assistance in the development of recommendations based on the reports.

> The assessment team will use the following criteria for the on-site evaluations. . . . The evaluator will develop a survey instrument to collect data regarding the perceptions held by the three main participatory groups in the project: students, teachers, and parents. The results of the surveys will be analyzed in combination with the interview, on-site observations, and the results of the summative evaluation.

2.   Summative Evaluation

A summative, or final, evaluation assesses the project accomplishments. It measures the achievement of stated objectives at the end of the project year. Funders want reports of measured changes or progress effected by the project—assurance that their money has been well spent.

The following proposal excerpt is from a summative evaluation design:

> The summative evaluation will provide information on the achievement of the stated objectives of the program outlined below, along with the procedures that will be used.
>
> > Objective IA: Increase the rate of students meeting the minimum expectations on the Texas Assessment of Academic Skills (TAAS) test.
> >
> > Procedure: In October, the evaluator will use district and school enrollment records to identify program participants. Participant lists at the beginning of the program will be matched with those at the end of each year of the project. In October 1996 and 1997, the evaluator will use enrollment records to identify program participants for the second and third year. . . .
>
> The evaluator will establish a matrix to report the impact of the program on academic achievement. The appropriate achievement data will be assigned to each cell of the matrix. Data will be disaggregated and performance of students will be charted. The evaluator will develop a matrix for each school during each year of the project.

C.   Data Collection Methods

Quantitative and qualitative methods are the two approaches that can be used to collect data. The choice depends upon the questions to be answered and the information requirements of those asking the questions. In many cases, a combination of the two methods will lead to the best results.

1. Quantitative Data Collection

Quantitative methods distill real-life activities into units that can be counted, measured, and manipulated statistically. Applicable data analysis techniques, which allow inferences regarding cause-and-effect relationships, include both descriptive statistics (e.g., averages, means, percentiles, frequency distributions) and inferential statistics (e.g., tests, simple linear regressions, chi-squares).

Mim Carlson has noted that quantitative methods are best when the questions involve:

- understanding the quantities of particular aspects of a program (e.g., number of student enrollees, number of dropouts);

- determining if a cause-and-effect relationship does occur;

- comparing two different methods that are seeking to achieve the same outcomes; and

- establishing numerical baselines, pretests, posttests, and a six-month or one-year follow-up.

2. Qualitative Data Collection

Qualitative methods are best when the questions involve:

- understanding the feelings or opinions regarding a program on the part of participants, staff, or the community;

- gaining insight into how the patterns of relationships within the program unfold;

- gathering multiple perspectives to understand the whole; and

- identifying approximate indicators that clients are moving in the right direction.

D. Evaluation Teams

Funding sources rely upon evaluators, whether internal or external teams (or teams composed of both), to objectively and accurately assess a project's effectiveness in achieving stated goals. When selecting evaluators, experience and expertise should be primary criteria.

1. Internal Evaluation Teams

Grantseekers sometimes decide to form an evaluation team using only members from their organization. They make this decision for a variety of reasons. Funder evaluation requirements may be simple and straightforward. Employees of the organization may have adequate experience and expertise in conducting the evaluation process.

However, sole reliance upon internal evaluators should not be decided by default. Funding agencies sometimes issue requests for proposals just weeks before submission deadlines. Inexperienced grantseekers, unaware that most government grant cycles repeat yearly, are often unprepared and decide to forego using external evaluators because of time constraints. Grantseekers who learn about upcoming grants by researching potential funding sources—during the planning process and before issuance of requests for proposals—have more evaluation options, and typically achieve greater success in securing funds.

2. External Evaluation Teams

Though an ideal evaluation team should include both internal and external evaluators, contracting with evaluators outside the grantseeking organization has many benefits. Persons not involved in the organization's daily activities are likely to be more objective in evaluating the project than those directly involved in its implementation. Independent evaluators are also likely to be less biased because they have no vested interest in the success of the project. They can contribute expertise and effective approaches gained from previous participation in grant-funded activities and project evaluations.

College professors tend to be excellent external evaluators. They understand the role of educators and librarians in the grant development process and can employ the verbiage and format that attract grant funding. Professors will often assist in developing the evaluation design, sometimes without charge. The grantseeking organization can include stipends for evaluators in the proposal budget, thereby enabling professors to enjoy the financial benefits of participation in the project. It is not uncommon for professors to be simultaneously involved in several grant projects.

Professors participate in the grant process for many reasons. They enjoy working outside their institutions but still within the field of education. Collaboration with other educators provides opportunities for professors to interact directly with students and to keep abreast of current student culture and school curricula. Many professors are published authors who enjoy writing articles about grant-funded projects for professional journals. Furthermore, grantseeking success enhances a résumé or vita.

Networking is a useful way to locate evaluators. Teachers, librarians, and administrators have frequent opportunities to meet business consultants and higher-education personnel. Those who return to college for graduate or postgraduate studies become acquainted with the faculty and can match projects being developed by their organizations against faculty expertise. Many former educators, including retirees, establish grant-related consulting businesses, including staff development and evaluation services.

Requests for applications issued by funders often indicate that priority status will be given to applicants who collaborate with parents (of school children), community members, business partners, and universities. These individuals serve as advisors, mentors, and evaluators. A proposal specifying effective collaboration conveys both the confidence of the individuals who will conduct the proposed project and the stability of the organization.

7

After the Proposal

A. Constructive Activities for the Interim Period Prior to the Notification of Grant Award (NOGA)

After the proposal has been submitted to the funder, the abrupt change in momentum can cause a post–project development malaise. Consider the following information and suggestions while awaiting a decision from the funding agency:

The time between proposal submission and award notification varies from a few weeks to many months (for state and federal grants, the average wait is about three months). In the request for application, the funder usually includes a timeline of events that designates the date of award notification. For a number of reasons, though, award notification seldom occurs exactly as scheduled. The funder may be inundated with many more proposals than anticipated. In such cases, the funder must employ reading panelists to review additional proposals, or appoint additional reading panelists.

The time required to thoroughly review and score a grant proposal increases with the complexity of the project and the length of the proposal. Many federal grants are offered for three to five years; proposals for such grants incorporate objectives, activities, budgets, and so on, for each year. Consequently, the reviewer must devote more time to consider components of the proposal.

Furthermore, problems beyond the funder's control often occur. Panelists, like most people, receive summons for jury duty, become ill, or have accidents. Weather can delay the review process as well. For example, during the mid-1990s, a winter blizzard forced government offices in Washington, D.C., to close for several days.

Pursuing other constructive activities during the waiting period will help the project team remain patient. For example, the project director might use this interlude to reflect on the implications of both success and failure:

- What if the grant is not received?

- Where else might funding for this project be secured?

- What are the immediate responsibilities of a grant recipient?

- What will be required of the project director?

- Assuming success, what can be accomplished while awaiting notification?

- Assuming failure, what can be accomplished while awaiting notification?

Refrain from contacting the funding agency unless additional information is requested. From the release of the request for application, through the deadline for submitting the proposal, the grantseeking organization generally is encouraged to direct questions to the funding agency when necessary. However, the funder may require that questions be submitted in writing. To remain impartial, most funders send a copy of each question, with answer, to all grantseekers who ordered an application packet.

Grantseekers should use the services of their organization's grants office (if one exists) as an intermediary in the communication process. This office may already be in close contact with the funding agency if others within the organization are also submitting proposals there.

The communication channels surrounding the Notification of Grant Award may vary from one situation to another. The chief administrator of the grant-seeking organization (e.g., superintendent for a public school district, director for a public library) usually receives the official notification-of-award letter, or letter of denial, for the proposal. The organization's grants office (if one exists) is contacted next. The project initiator and other appropriate project personnel are then notified. In some cases, however, the funding agency will contact the project director first. If so, higher officials in the chain of command should be informed immediately.

Whether the grant is awarded or denied, the grants office should obtain proposal scores and reviewer comments from the funder and forward this information to the project initiator. Government funding agencies are typically required by law to forward this information about the proposal to applicants and, accordingly, will do so without waiting for a formal request. Such feedback will likely prove beneficial in future efforts to secure grant funding.

B.   Strategies for Successful Grant Recipients

1.   Actions Immediately Following the Notification of Grant Award

If funding for the proposal is secured, the first order of business should be to celebrate! Hard work deserves to be rewarded. However, everyone involved in the grant project should realize that writing the proposal is merely the precursor to actually conducting the project. Before the punch glasses have been shelved in anticipation of the next success, the grant recipient should already be laying the foundation for the partnership with the funder. All key personnel should understand that the official who signs the proposal is legally binding the grantee organization to conduct the project as proposed; therefore, that administrator expects everyone mentioned in the proposal to help shoulder the load of responsibility. Implementation of the project must begin on time; objectives must be met according to the timeline; and reports must be submitted to the funder in a timely manner.

A recent event illustrates the negative repercussions of failing to adequately plan for the receipt of a grant award. A few days after a high school principal received a Notification of Grant Award, more grant documentation surfaced in his daily mail. He filed it with his copy of the proposal and promptly forgot about it. Six months later, the superintendent of the school district received a letter from the funder indicating that a quarterly report was overdue. The superintendent visited the school, where an embarrassed principal discovered that those hastily filed papers were instructions and forms for the quarterly grant reports.

2.   Guidelines for the Negotiation Process Between the Funder and Grant Recipient

To avoid such unfortunate occurrences, the following checklist should prove useful in framing the negotiation process:

a.   Ask for the names of the funding officers who will address project and financial issues. Establish a rapport with them.

b.   Ask what amount of funding (exactly) will be awarded, including indirect costs. The project director may become involved in a protracted dialogue with the funding agency beginning immediately after the award announcement.

c.   Ask what reports will be required and what terms and conditions must be followed.

d.   Ask when the funds will be sent and, if necessary, revise project start and end dates accordingly.

e.   Ask what method of payment the funder will use and what financial forms must be completed.

f.   Ask when grant funds can be spent, and when cash advances can be requested.

g.   Ask if a signed letter of acceptance is required.

h.   If the funder reduces the project budget, counter with related cuts in project objectives and activities.

i.   If the budget or project must be changed, consult with project staff and administrators.

j.   If the budget or project is changed, send the funder a written explanation.

k.   If letters of support from congressional representatives are needed, ask the grants coordinator (or the official acting in a similar capacity) for assistance.

l.   Ask the grants coordinator for any assistance needed in the negotiation process.

3.   Project Implementation

Project implementation should begin within 30 days of receiving the funder's award notice. Immediately after receiving notification of the award, the project director should do the following:

a.   Send a thank-you letter to the funder. A funder who awards a grant and then never again hears from the organization (except perhaps in cases where reporting updates are required) until more funding is being sought is unlikely to provide additional support. Funders, especially foundations and corporations, file thank-you letters for future reference. If the grant recipient is a board of trustees or directors, take photographs of two or three people (e.g., a school principal, the project director, and a teacher or librarian) and send them as part of a press release to local newspapers. Then attach the newspaper article to the thank-you letter. Funders often include letters and pictures from grant recipients in their publications (e.g., annual reports).

b.   Ask an appropriate official to sign the grant agreement, if necessary. In cases where the recipient is a public school district, the superintendent's signature is usually required.

c.   Seek help from the personnel department in filling grant-funded positions. Supply well-defined job descriptions. Meet with an officer from the department to clarify the nature of your line authority—and responsibilities—with respect to project employees.

d.   Publicize the award internally and within the community. Such communication should be worded to derive maximum public relations value. Be vigilant to potential criticism; prepare carefully worded rejoinders well in advance of anticipated controversies.

e.   Write purchase requisitions to order equipment and supplies. The preliminary investigations regarding price and availability should have been conducted prior to notification of the grant award. In cases where the recipient normally requires strict adherence to a bid process, negotiations for obtaining exemptions should be conducted as soon as possible. If the bid process cannot be bypassed, make arrangements to ensure that the process proceeds as efficiently as possible.

f.   Establish initial subcontracting arrangements, if necessary. Conduct investigations of eligible organizations to determine whether or not they are capable of fulfilling requirements.

g.   Establish project administration procedures and a related timeline, including a schedule for completion of reports and forms.

h.   Meet with advisory committee members, project staff, and project evaluators to coordinate the activities and timeline.

Shortly before the receipt of grant funds, the project director should speak to the appropriate higher official within the organization about the requisition process and purchasing policies. Prepare vendor requisitions, but do not submit them until grant funds have arrived. Arrange for project facilities and equipment. If the project requires renovation of facilities, the recipient organization may allow funding from other allocations until grant funding arrives.

The person responsible for hiring grant-funded personnel should interview staff candidates sent by the personnel department. If many candidates apply, the interview process may prove time-consuming. Rather than risk delaying project implementation, interviews and hiring should be conducted while waiting for grant funds to arrive. It would be wise, particularly from a legal standpoint, to advise candidates that job availability is contingent upon grant funding. An answer should be prepared for candidates who will ask how the organization plans to fund the position after the grant money has been spent. Those who ask this question demonstrate at least some familiarity with the grantseeking process.

As soon as the funds arrive, the project director can begin drafting consultant contracts, submitting vendor requisitions, and establishing facilities and equipment. The director should also formalize the hiring of staff and, because several months will have passed since proposal submission, assemble all key personnel to review the proposal. Discuss duties and responsibilities. Remember that most personnel already have full-time jobs and will be assuming additional duties through their involvement with the project. Establish a schedule for project staff to begin and complete activities. Discuss the plan for monitoring activities and the timeline, as well as documentation and the evaluation of activities and personnel.

Alert personnel to the importance of two-way communication during the project. Personnel should be expected to notify the project director when something goes awry, and should feel comfortable about consulting the project director or an appropriate higher official within the organization if any questions arise regarding project implementation procedures. If circumstances prevent activities from proceeding as scheduled, it will be necessary to adjust the project calendar. Emphasize the importance of following the plans set forth in the proposal.

Many professionals, including teachers and librarians, are unaccustomed to assuming an active role in handling funds, particularly in large amounts. They are usually apprehensive about procedures for handling grant funds. A Texas teacher, also serving as a project director, upon learning from the district's grants coordinator that he would be responsible for requisitioning materials and writing checks, exclaimed, "Gee, I've never been permitted to handle an object sharper than a pencil before!"

The project director should schedule a meeting with the organization's financial officer to discuss the disbursement of grant funds. Prior to the meeting, a copy of the grant proposal should have been sent to the financial officer. The project director should take all grant proposal budget worksheets to the meeting, as well as documents received from the funder.

The financial officer will instruct the project director regarding procedures for managing the budget. Detailed records of each transaction should be kept. A typical project may encompass a more complex array of activities than the director thought possible at the outset. For instance, grants often provide funding for staff (e.g., teachers) to attend conferences in remote locations, and for project clients (e.g., students) to participate in field trips. Such activities will require the project director to learn how to prepare and submit expense reports.

Financial procedures will be new to most first-time grant recipients. Project participants should review and discuss them with the financial officer until they are confident they understand the organization's expectations and the funder's reporting requirements.

Table 7-1 summarizes important tasks for the project director.

Table 7-1

**Preparations for Successful Implementation
of a Grant Project**

To ensure the success of the project, the project director should conform to a number of established business procedures. Upon receipt of the award notice, the director should:

1. Meet with the appropriate official from the organization to discuss the management of project funds.

2. Submit to the organization's main office grant proposal budget worksheets and other materials related to initial administration of the grant.

3. Obtain and review procedures for

   a. creating the budget;

   b. spending funds;

   c. keeping detailed records of each transaction; and

   d. preparing expense reports.

Upon receipt of the funds, the director should:

1. Forward to the organization's main office the check or entitlement card from the funding agency and all grant documentation.

2. Review all documentation with appropriate official from the organization to ensure compliance with all grant requirements.

C. Strategies for Organizations Failing to Obtain Grant Funding

Organizations participating in the grant development process for any appreciable length of time will inevitably experience the disappointment of a failed proposal. An experienced grants officer observed, "The only people I know who have a 100% success rate in grantseeking are those who have written just one proposal and had the good fortune to receive funding!" As unfair as it might seem to proposal writers, good proposals do not always attract money. In some cases, the funder simply does not have sufficient resources to subsidize all deserving applicants.

Notification that a project will not be funded is not a personal rejection, nor does it signify that grantseeking should be abandoned. Consider the proposal writing process to be a positive growth experience, even when funding is denied. Knowledge gained in the process will contribute to better proposals and future success in obtaining funding. If the funder sends a letter of denial, review the reasons for the denial. Send a copy of the letter to your organization's grants office (if one exists). State and federal grant funding agencies will send applicants a card containing the document control number. Send a copy of this card to the grants office.

The grants office should contact the funding agency and obtain proposal scores and reviewer comments. This information will provide insight into the proposal's strengths and weaknesses. The grant development team should be assembled to review the scores and comments. Discuss how to rewrite and strengthen the components that received low scores. Determining the weaknesses in a proposal is an important learning experience and will contribute to future success.

Belcher and Jacobsen have noted that it generally is productive to supplement the funder's scores and comments with a self-appraisal process built around the following questions:

- How pressing a need does the project fill?

- Does the proposal demonstrate a clear anticipation of problems that are likely to occur, and an awareness of relevant scholarship and available resources?

- How does the applicant's background clearly qualify him or her to carry out this project successfully?

- Is the budget sound?

- In general, does the proposal have promise of making a significant contribution?

Poor Grantsmanship Practices

Eventual success is likely to depend upon the ability of the grantseeker to develop consistently high standards in the proposal writing process. Consequently, the inclination to engage in poor grantsmanship practices must be overcome. Poor grantsmanship practices generally beget poor results. Table 7-2 is a concise list of practices to be avoided.

Table 7-2

Poor Grantsmanship Practices

1. Failure to research the potential funder.

2. Failure to follow the funder's guidelines.

3. Failure to follow the basic rules of proposal writing.

4. Missing signatures.

5. Missing components.

6. Failure to meet the proposal deadline.

7. Failure to comply with the prescribed page limit.

8. Lack of attention to detail.

9. Dull, uninteresting writing; timid, unimaginative proposals.

10. Use of undefined acronyms.

11. Verbose language; overuse of jargon and "educationese."

12. Unjustified requests for technology.

13. Unrealistic needs statement.

14. Budget items not included in the project description.

15. Padded or mathematically incorrect budget.

16. Numerous errors in spelling, grammar, and punctuation.

17. Fonts that are visually unappealing or too small.

18. Complicated, confusing passages.

19. Failure to convey clarity of purpose.

20. Lack of collaboration.

21. Failure to describe project management capability.

Failure to research the potential funder can lead to an unproductive effort. The grantseeker must investigate what a particular funder will—and will not—fund. For example, regardless of how attractive a fine arts proposal might be, a local oil company committed to environmental projects will certainly reject it. The oil company's administration and proposal reviewers would admonish the grantseeker for insufficient homework.

"Those who have the gold make the rules." Failure to follow the funder's guidelines is likely to result in a failure to attract grant funding. The primary purpose of guidelines is to facilitate efficient review of the proposal by reading panelists. However, even seemingly minor or idiosyncratic guidelines must be followed. If the funder requests that submissions not employ fancy bindings or colored paper, for example, the proposal should be submitted on white paper stapled together in the upper left corner. One funder divulged that he required proposals to follow an A-C-B format, rather than the usual A-B-C format. He instructed his secretary to check each proposal that arrived and discard those that did not follow his prescribed format. He reasoned that anyone who did not follow his instructions probably would not handle his money wisely. Successful grantseekers typically study and review guidelines several times before beginning the writing process.

The basic rules of proposal writing include the use of a straightforward presentation style and coherent organization scheme. Avoid digressions that fail to directly address the concerns of the funding agency.

A missing signature will guarantee a rejected proposal. It indicates to the funder that the key personnel in the grantseeking organization do not properly attend to detail. It may also indicate that the school district superintendent, library director, or other official responsible for approving proposals was unaware of the proposal and the fact that it was being submitted to a funding agency. Funders frequently request that blue ink be used, to facilitate identification of original signatures. The project director (or a delegated representative) should highlight instructions of this nature while reviewing the request for application.

A missing component, especially a major component, may result in a rejected proposal. To ensure that a proposal is complete, compile a checklist of inclusions prior to beginning the writing process.

The deadline for submittal is not negotiable. It should be the first date established in the project calendar. The timeline should be realistic, and should ensure completion of the proposal well in advance of the deadline. Some funders require that proposals arrive at their offices by 5:00 P.M. on the deadline date. Others require that proposals be postmarked on or before the deadline date.

Proposals that exceed a prescribed page limit are rarely funded. In fact, some organizations check the number of pages as soon as the proposal arrives. If it exceeds the stated page limitation, it is discarded—unread. One funder stated, "If I say I want 25 pages, I stop reading when I've read 25 pages. If I haven't read a complete proposal by then, the writer can forget about receiving a grant from us."

A lack of attention to detail may result in a rejected proposal. If the applicant overlooks simple things, such as numbering pages or defining all acronyms, the funder might well assume that project personnel, if funded by a grant, would not properly attend to the details of the proposed project.

It is imperative that the proposal communicate a sense of excitement and commitment to achieving project goals. Dull writing undercuts any effort at instilling such a picture. The proposal should be proactive in tone as opposed to hesitant in approach.

Verbose language and overuse of jargon and "educationese" (language that only professional educators would be likely to understand) are risky. Reviewers generally do not award high points to proposals that annoy them.

Seeking a grant for the sole purpose of purchasing technology is a common mistake. Funders do not want to invest in equipment; they want to solve problems or provide services. However, funders will consider a proposal that requests funding for the technology necessary to conduct a useful project.

A needs statement specifying more needs than one grant can fulfill is uninviting for a funder. One funder observed, "If a school sends me a proposal that tries to address every problem of every student through one program, I know they haven't spent enough time planning. If I can't see where my money will make a real impact—a real difference, then I'll move on to the next proposal."

The budget should reflect the project description; it should not contain any surprises. Upon discovering a substantial item that is not mentioned in the project description, the funder will likely assume that the applicant is attempting to use the grant as a purchasing ploy, without regard for the proposed project.

Funders are quick to detect a padded budget. Inexperienced proposal writers are sometimes ineffective in their research and either estimate or boost prices. At best, the writer will be perceived as lazy; at worst, the writer will be perceived as dishonest. In either case, the proposal is unlikely to result in a grant. Incorrect budget computations indicate a lack of attention to detail. If the proposal is being produced with computer software, use the calculator feature to perform computations. If not, use a manual calculator or an adding machine.

Numerous errors in spelling, grammar, and punctuation are likely to distract the reviewer from the information contained in the proposal. The importance of proofreading cannot be overemphasized. The proposal should be proofread at least twice, the second time by someone possessing strong spelling and language skills, as well as a reputation for thorough, conscientious work.

Fonts that are visually unappealing or too small will detract from the proposal's content. They also cause eyestrain for the reader. Though some fonts (e.g., Olde English) may be beautiful to look at, the eyes rapidly tire after reading more than a few words. The best font choices are economical and straightforward in appearance—Ariel, Garamond, Times New Roman, and Courier. Small print may also cause the reader to engage in skimming, thereby increasing the likelihood that key points will be missed. The preferred font sizes are generally 12- or 14-point.

Complicated, confusing passages result in a loss of points and, often, a rejected proposal. Simplicity of presentation and economy of language create understandable information. In addition, alternative forms of packaging information (e.g., graphs, charts, and timetables that incorporate objectives, dates, activities, key personnel, instruments and methods of evaluation, etc.) can create a more efficient proposal.

Some proposals fail to convey clarity of purpose. For instance, the following goal appeared in a proposal: ". . . to provide an outstanding, state-of-the-art program where students achieve academically." Such statements leave the reader wondering, What is the real purpose of the program? What do the project personnel want to achieve? Vague wording and jargon seriously compromise a proposal's chances of success.

Funders today expect collaboration among all stakeholders. Funders providing resources for education expect the involvement of parents, community members, the business community, nonprofit organizations, and institutions of higher learning. Funders awarding grants to collaboratives of large numbers of schools or, in some cases, school districts has been a major trend in the late 1990s.

Failure to describe project management capability typically results in a failure to attract funding. This description is the place to promote previous grant success. A project that will be directed by someone with past experience in grant management has an advantage over a project that will be staffed by only inexperienced personnel. However, inexperience can be countered by describing previous assignments that required skills and competencies relevant to management.

Resubmitting the Proposal and Seeking Other Funding Sources

In the event that money again becomes available from the same source, revise the proposal and resubmit it during the next funding cycle. Grantseekers frequently receive funding upon second submission of the proposal. A National Endowment for the Humanities (NEH) staff member recently noted that almost 90 percent of resubmissions to the NEH library program have been funded. At the same time, chances of success will be substantially increased by searching for additional sources of funding for the project.

Implementing the strategies discussed in this section will increase the tangible assets that remain after a failure to obtain grant funding. These include a well-organized project proposal and potentially useful professional contacts. If the proposal cannot be resubmitted to a particular funding agency, the project officer may be able to recommend other sources. In some cases, the officer may offer to act as intermediary in contacting other funders. Grantseekers should remember that, no matter how good the proposal, factors outside their control may play a role in failure to obtain funding. Each funder possesses a limited amount of money. In addition, many strive for geographic balance when disbursing funds.

As a final resort, explore the possibility of obtaining other sources of funding. Most educational institutions possess discretionary funds for disbursement as needed. Friends groups can be helpful in raising both money and community awareness of the project's inherent potential. Philanthropists who profess interest in the project's stated goals may also be able to provide needed assistance. If the proposal has merit, do not abandon it.

APPENDICES

APPENDICES

A
Annotated Bibliography

This list of resources is by no means exhaustive. It has been compiled based on the recommendations of educators working in the area of seeking and administering grants. Few resources published prior to 1990 have been included. Though all these resources have components related to education, not all specifically or exclusively concern libraries. For Internet/World Wide Web sites, and for many of the resources related to funding sources, annotations have been provided to clarify their content and scope. Internet/World Wide Web addresses (URLs) may change; new sites are continuously established, and established sites, for a variety of reasons, may be modified or discontinued entirely. Browse sites, follow links, and maintain contacts with others in the field with whom you can exchange "new finds."

Tools for Discovering Funding Sources

Print Resources

Annual Register of Grant Support. Indianapolis, IN: Marquis Who's Who, 1969– . Annual.

> Education-related sources are included in this listing of organizations offering grant support.

Bauer, David G. *The Complete Grants Sourcebook for Higher Education.* 3d ed. Phoenix, AZ: American Council on Education/Oryx, 1995.

> Surveys the entire grantseeking process, with an emphasis on the university environment.

——. *The "How To" Grants Manual: Successful Grantseeking Techniques for Obtaining Public and Private Grants.* 3d ed. Phoenix, AZ: American Council on Education/Oryx, 1995.

> Offers practical insights for prospective grantseekers, covering all stages of the search for funding.

Belcher, Jane C., and Julia M. Jacobsen. *From Idea to Funded Project: Grant Proposals That Work.* Phoenix, AZ: Oryx, 1992.

> Though directed primarily to the small liberal arts college, this resource provides a thorough discussion of the entire grantseeking process. An annotated bibliography is included.

Bernhard, Elizabeth A., Jody Feder, and Alvin C. Lin, eds. *1996 Guide to Federal Funding for Education.* Arlington, VA: Educational Funding Research Council, 1996.

The Big Book of Library Grant Money . . . . Chicago: American Library Association, 1994– . Annual.

> Focuses on private and corporate foundations, as well as direct corporate donors with a proven record of funding libraries. Lists grant sources by state, has extensive indexing, and includes an annotated bibliography and a section titled "Library Fundraising on the Web."

Brewer, Ernest W., Charles M. Achilles, and Jay R. Fuhriman. *Finding Funding, Grantwriting and Project Management from Start to Finish.* 2d ed. Thousand Oaks, CA: Corwin, 1995.

> Provides a comprehensive analysis of the grantseeking process and the administering of funded projects.

Carlson, Mim. *Winning Grants Step by Step: Support Centers of America's Complete Workbook for Planning, Developing, and Writing Successful Proposals.* San Francisco: Jossey-Bass, 1995.

A systematic guide for transforming an idea that requires funding into a proposal that merits funding.

Catalog of Federal Domestic Assistance. Washington, DC: Superintendent of Documents, U.S. Government Printing Office.

Lists all federal programs and includes a useful index.

Chelekis, George. *The Action Guide to Government Grants, Loans and Giveaways: A Home Study Course.* Clearwater, FL: Rex, 1990.

A straightforward introduction to federal funding sources.

Corporate 500: Directory of Corporate Philanthropy. San Francisco: Public Management Institute, 1982/83– . Annual.

Includes sections titled "Grants-at-a-Glance" and "Corporate Philanthropy Online."

Directory of Research Grants. Phoenix, AZ: Oryx, 1975– . Annual.

Includes a listing of grants available through educational institutions, as well as foundations and private sources. Includes the section "A Guide to Proposal Planning and Writing" by Lynn E. Miner.

Dumochel, Rovert. *Government Assistance Almanac.* 10th ed. Detroit, MI: Omnigraphics, 1996.

A selection of entries from the *Catalog of Federal Domestic Assistance*, but with supplementary tables and lists.

Federal Register. Washington, DC: Superintendent of Documents, U.S. Government Printing Office, 1936– . Daily.

Publishes grant announcements and pending changes in rules and regulations. Check the nearest federal depository library to locate this and other relevant documents published by U.S. government agencies. The *Federal Register* is also available on the World Wide Web at http://www.access.gpo.gov/su_docs/.

Foundation Directory. New York: The Foundation Center, 1960– . Annual.

Covers the funding community and private foundations that have assets of at least $1 million or that offer grant awards of at least $100,000. A supplement covers foundations that offer grants ranging from $25,000 to $99,999.

Foundation Grants Index. New York: The Foundation Center, 1970/71– . Annual.

> Describes the funding interests and priorities of foundations, including brief data about type and amount of previous awards.

Grants and Awards for Teachers. 2d ed. Alexandria, VA: Capitol Publications, 1996.

> One of Capitol's numerous publications related to grants and fundraising.

Guide to U.S. Foundations. New York: The Foundation Center, 1993– . Annual.

> Lists all U.S. foundations currently offering grants. This is one of several resources published by The Foundation Center, which may be contacted directly at 79 Fifth Avenue, New York, NY 10003; 1-800-424-9836.

Hall, Mary S. *Getting Funded: A Complete Guide to Proposal Writing.* 3rd ed. Portland, OR: Continuing Education Publishers, Portland State University, 1988.

Lefferts, Robert. *Getting a Grant in the 1990s: How to Write Successful Grant Proposals.* New York: Prentice-Hall, 1990.

> An excellent overview of grantseeking, supplemented by several appendices ("Sample Program Proposal and Critique," "The Foundation Center Cooperating Collections Network," and "Bibliography of State and Local Foundation Directories"), a glossary, and an index.

Locke, Lawrence F., Waneen Wyrick Spirduso, and Stephen J. Silverman. *Proposals That Work: A Guide for Planning Dissertations and Grant Proposals.* 3d ed. Newbury Park, CA: Sage, 1993.

National Guide to Funding for Libraries and Information Services. 3d ed. New York: The Foundation Center, 1996.

> One of a series published by The Foundation Center. Other titles in the series include *National Guide to Funding for Elementary and Secondary Education* (1996); *National Guide to Funding for Children, Youth, and Families* (1996); *National Guide to Funding for Women and Girls* (1996); and *National Guide to Foundation Funding in Higher Education* (1989).

Quick, James A., ed. *Grant Seeker's Directory of K–12 Funders.* Greenville, SC: Polaris, 1966.

Schumacher, Dorin. *Get Funded! A Practical Guide for Scholars Seeking Research Support from Business.* Newbury Park, CA: Sage, 1992.

Shellow, Jill R., and Nancy C. Stella, eds. *Grant Seekers Guide.* 3d ed. New York: Bell, 1989.

Sponsored by the National Network of Grantmakers, this resource provides a concise overview of the grantseeking process.

Internet/World Wide Web Sites

American Library Association. *American Association of School Librarians.* © 1998. Available: http://www.ala.org/aasl/index.html (Accessed December 7, 1998).

Provides information about the American Association of School Librarians (AASL) and its programs, as well as links to sites related to library media services.

Apple Computer, Inc. *Apple Partners in Education.* © 1998. Available: http://ed.info. apple.com/education/ (Accessed December 7, 1998).

Click on "Apple in Education" to browse "Educational Grants."

The Foundation Center. *The Foundation Center.* ©1995–1998. Available: http:// fdncenter.org (Accessed December 7, 1998).

Includes information about funders and funding trends.

Government Publications Office. *Federal Register.* © October 1, 1998. Available: http://www.access.gpo.gov/su_docs/favor.html (Accessed December 7, 1998).

See annotation for print version.

Hewlett-Packard Co. *U.S. Philanthropy.* © 1998. Available: http://webcenter.hp. com.grants/us/index.html (Accessed December 14, 1998).

From here link to descriptions of Hewlett-Packard's charitable activities related to K–12 Education.

McRel. August 13, 1998. *Mathematics and Science Education Resources.* © 1998. Available: http://www.mcrel.org/resources/links/funding.asp (Accessed December 8, 1998).

Along with program information are links to helpful standards, curriculum, and assessment information.

Mendell, Joy. *Grants Central Station.* Available: http://house-of-hope.org/grants-central-station.htm (Accessed December 7, 1998).

Provides access to information about state and federal grants (including the *Catalog of Federal Domestic Assistance* and the *Federal Register*), as well as information about tutorials and workshops concerning grants and proposal writing.

National Endowment for the Humanities. Available: http://www.neh.fed.us/ (Accessed December 8, 1998).

Look here for links to information about what types of projects the National Endowment for the Humanities (NEH) funds, criteria for eligibility, and how to apply.

Scholastic, Inc. *Electronic Learning.* © 1998, 97. Available: http://scholastic.com/EL (Accessed December 7, 1998).

Provides a grants update and descriptions of funded projects.

TGCI. *The Grantsmanship Center.* Available: http://www.tgci.com/ (Accessed December 8, 1998).

Offers a varied menu, including "Nonprofit Resources," "Grantsmanship Training," and "Fundraising Training," as well as current *Federal Register* grant announcements.

University of Pennsylvania Library. October 17, 1998. *Penn Library Grants and Research.* © 1998. Available: http://www.library.upenn.edu/resources/reference/general/grants/grants.html (Accessed December 8, 1998).

Provides links to funder Web sites, as well as to information provided by foundations, including application procedures.

U.S. Department of Education. *National Library of Education.* November 4, 1998. Available: http://www.ed.gov/NLE/ (Accessed December 8, 1998).

U.S. Department of Education. December 7, 1998. *National Science Foundation.* Available: http://www.nsf.gov/ (Accessed December 8, 1998).

The link to "Grants/Funding/Program Areas" includes a grant proposal guide and full text of the *NSF Grant Policy Manual.*

U.S. Department of Education Office of Educational Technology. August 3, 1998. *Resource Guide to Federal Funding for Technology in Education.* Available: http://www.ed.gov/Technology/ (Accessed December 8, 1998).

Includes sources of funding for hardware and software.

U.S. Department of Education Office of Educational Technology. *U.S. Department of Education.* Available: http://gopher.ed.gov./ (Accessed December 8, 1998).

"Money Matters" links to information about (ED) guidelines and regulations, as well as a section titled "What Should I Know About ED Grants?"

U.S. Department of Education Office of Educational Technology. December 4, 1998. *U.S. Department of Education Secretary's Initiatives.* Available: http://inet.ed.gov/inits.html (Accessed December 8, 1998).

Browse this site for information about how to make use of the School Construction Initiative and the Elementary and Secondary Education Act.

U.S. Department of Education Office of Educational Technology. *U.S. Department of Education Technology Initiatives*. Available: http://inet.ed.gov/Technology/ (Accessed December 9, 1998).

> Explore the availability of state grants under the Technology Literacy Challenge Fund, Challenge Grants for Technology in Education and look at the "Resource Guide to Federal Funding for Technology in Education."

Other Online Resources

The Foundation Center. 1999. *Foundation Directory*. Annual updates through DIALOG (File 26).

> See annotation for print version.

The Foundation Center. 1973 to date. *Foundation Grants Index*. Quarterly updates through DIALOG (File 27).

> See annotation for print version.

Oryx Press. 1999. *Grants*. Monthly updates through DIALOG (File 85).

> This database provides information about funders and grant opportunities in the public and private sectors.

Tools to Support the Project (from Initiation to Evaluation)

Print Resources

Ally, Brian. "Gifts, Grants and Strings [Hidden Costs of Fund Raising]." *Technicalities* 13 (June 1993): 1.

Applied Research & Development Institute and Support Centers of America. *Successful Proposal Writing Workshop*. University Heights, OH: Nonprofit Partners, 1995.

Bayley, Linda. "Grant Me This: How to Write a Winning Grant Proposal." *School Library Journal* 41 (September 1995): 126–28.

Carlson, Mim. *Winning Grants Step by Step*. San Francisco: Jossey-Bass, 1995.

Effective Evaluation: A Systematic Approach for Grantseekers and Project Managers. Alexandria, VA: Capitol Publications, 1995.

The Effective Grant Office: Streamlining Grants Development and Management.
Alexandria, VA: Capitol Publications, 1995.

Ferguson, Jacqueline, and Michael Gershowitz. *The Grantseeker's Answer Book.*
Alexandria, VA: Capitol Publications, 1995.

The Foundation Center's User-Friendly Guide: A Grantseeker's Guide to Resources.
3d ed. New York: The Foundation Center, 1994.

Frost, Gordon Jay, ed. *Winning Grant Proposals.* University Heights, OH: Nonprofit
Partners, 1995.

Geever, Jane C., and Patricia McNeill. *The Foundation Center's Guide to Proposal
Writing.* New York: The Foundation Center, 1993.

Goals 2000 and Title I: How the Two Programs Interact. Arlington, VA: Education
Funding Research Council, 1996.

Goldberg, Susan. "Alternate Funding Sources: Corporate Funding: Finding New
Partners." *Bottom Line* 4 (winter 1990): 33–37.

Gothberg, Helen M., and Edith H. Ferrell. "New Sources on Grants and Grant Writing." *Reference Services Review* 21 (1993): 17–30.

Grants Development Kit. Alexandria, VA: Capitol Publications, 1996.

Grants Management Kit. Alexandria, VA: Capitol Publications, 1996.

The Grantseeker's Guide to Project Evaluations. Alexandria, VA: Capitol Publications, 1995.

Guide to Funding Databases & Resources Online. Arlington, VA: Education Research Funding Council, 1996.

Hale, Phale D., Jr. *Writing Grant Proposals That Win!* Alexandria, VA: Capitol Publications, 1995.

Holden, Carolyn. "Grants: Bonus or Bother?" *The School Librarian's Workshop* 11
(January 1991): 2–3.

How to Win More Grant$. Arlington, VA: Education Research Funding Council,
1996.

Karges-Bone, Linda. *Grant Writing for Teachers: If You Can Write a Lesson Plan, You Can Write a Grant.* Carthage, IL: Good Apple, 1994.

Kaye, R. "Get Going with Grants." [presented at the Preconference Institute on the Nineties Imperative] *School Librarian's Workshop* 14 (January 1994): 9–10; and 14 (February 1994): 13–14.

Kollasch, Matthew. "School Media Matters: Grant World; It Pays to Play." *Wilson Library Bulletin* 67 (March 1993): 68.

Kussrow, Paul G., and Helen Laurence. "Instruction in Developing Grant Proposals: A Librarian-Faculty Partnership [Teaching Students How to Apply for Grant Funding and Write Proposals]." *Research Strategies* 11 (winter 1993): 47–51.

Meador, Roy. *Guidelines for Preparing Proposals.* 2d ed. Chelsea, MI: Lewis, 1991.

New, Cheryl Carter. *Proposal Development Tool Kit.* 3 vols. Greenville, SC: Polaris, 1995.

New, Cheryl Carter, and James A. Quick. *Grant Seeking Fundamentals Workshop Workbooks.* 2 vols. Greenville, SC: Polaris, 1996.

1996 Guide to Federal Funding for Education. Arlington, VA: Education Funding Research Council, 1996.

Norris, Dennis M. "Creating a Fundable Monster." *Electronic Learning* 15 (January/ February 1996): 20–21.

———. "Goal-Objectives-Activities: How to Translate the Grant Writing Mantra into Fundable English." *Electronic Learning* 15 (November/December 1995): 24–25.

Ogden, Thomas E., and Israel A. Goldberg. *Research Proposals: A Guide to Success.* 2d ed. New York: Raven Press, 1995.

Olson, David L. *Grantsmanship: A Primer for School Librarians.* Rev. ed. Farmington: University of Maine at Farmington Mantor Library, 41 High Street, 04938, 1991.

111 Secrets to Smarter Grantsmanship. Arlington, VA: Education Funding Research Council, 1996.

Orlich, Don. *Designing Successful Grant Proposals*. Alexandria, VA: Association for Supervision and Curriculum Development, 1996.

Phillips, Virginia. "Fund-Raising and Grantsmanship for the 1990's." *Texas Libraries* 51 (winter 1990/91): 118–23.

Quick, James A., ed. *Grant Seeker's Desk Reference*. Greenville, SC: Polaris, 1996.

Ratzlaff, Leslie, ed. *Education Grantwinners: Models of Effective Proposal Structure and Style*. Alexandria, VA: Capitol Publications, 1991.

Staerkel, Kathleen, comp., et al. *Youth Services Librarians as Managers: A How-to Guide from Budgeting to Personnel*. Chicago: American Library Association, 1995.

Strategies and Resources for Developing Quality Grant Applications. Oklahoma City: Oklahoma State Department of Education, 1995.

Sumerford, Steve, et al. "Careful Planning: The Fundraising Edge"; "Business-School Partnerships: Future Media Center Funding Sources"; "Rakin' in the Clams . . . Or, How to Make Lots of Cash from Renting Best-Sellers"; "The Book Business: The Bookstore as an Alternative Funding Source for the Public Library"; and "Friends of the Library Book Sales." *North Carolina Libraries* 53 (spring 1995): 3–17.

Title I Today: A Comprehensive Overview of the Largest Federal Aid Program for Local Schools. Arlington, VA: Education Funding Research Council, 1996.

Williams, Harold, Arthur Webb, and William Phillips. *Outcome Funding: A New Approach to Targeted Grantmaking*. University Heights, OH: Nonprofit Partners, 1995.

Winning Federal Grants: A Guide to the Government's Grant-Making Process. Alexandria, VA: Capitol Publications, 1995.

Workforce Development Training Proposals. Arlington, VA: Education Funding Research Council, 1996.

Internet/World Wide Web Sites

America Goes Back to School. September 8, 1998. Available: http://www.ed.gov/Family/agbts/ (Accessed December 8, 1998).

Information about how to involve families, businesses, other educational institutions, and the community in local schools and school reform.

American Association of School Administrators. December 7, 1998. Available: http://www.aasa.org/ (Accessed December 8, 1998).

Learn about American Association of School Administrators (AASA) programs and publications while reviewing AASA's topical legislative alerts.

American Association of School Librarians. 1998. Available: http://www.ala.org/ aasl/index.html (Accessed December 8, 1998).

Examine the AASL/AECT National Guidelines and AASL position statements, and learn about programs such as "ICONnect," "Count on Reading," and the "National Library Power Program."

Apple Support Information. 1998. Available: http://www.info.apple.com/ (Accessed December 8, 1998).

Click on "Support Index" for information about using and maintaining Macintosh computers.

Applied Research Center. November 18, 1998. *Applied Research Center.* Available: http://www.arc.org/ (Accessed December 8, 1998).

Learn about the programs, publications and activities of this "public policy, educational and research institute whose work emphasizes issues of race and social change."

The Arc Home Page. *ARC—Applied Research Center.* Available: http://the arc.org (Accessed December 8, 1998).

Includes information about grant resources, federally funded projects, assistive technology, and much more. The ARC deals with disabled persons.

Best Practices in Education. October 23, 1998. Available: http://www.bestpraceduc. org/ (Accessed December 8, 1998).

This page is sponsored by NAME, a nonprofit organization that researches effective educational practices in other countries and adapts them for use in the United States. Its goal is to combine "the best in international with the best in American teaching practice." The page describes currently funded programs as well.

Drummond, Tom. March 17, 1998. *NSCC Early Childhood Education.* Available: http://nsccux.sccd.ctc.edu/%7Eeceprog/ (Accessed December 8, 1998).

Sponsored by North Seattle Community College (NSCC), this site is designed to be "a resource for useful information for adults who lead, parent, care for, or teach children under the age of six."

U.S. Department of Agriculture. *Food and Nutrition Information Center.* Available: http://www.nal.usda.gov/fnic/ (Accessed December 8, 1998).

Learn about "Nutrition Education and Training (NET) Program Products," "Healthy School Meals Training Materials," dietary guidelines, and food and nutrition software and multimedia programs.

U.S. Department of Education. November 24, 1998. *ERIC.* Available: http://www.accesseric.org.81 (Accessed December 8, 1998).

Provides links to all ERIC (Education Resources Information Center) sites, options for searching the ERIC database, and access to the full text of ERIC Digests.

U.S. Department of Education. November 25, 1998. *News from ED.* Available: http://www.ed.gov/news.html (Accessed December 8, 1998).

This service from the U.S. Department of Education supplies "2–3 messages per week on reports, studies, funding opportunities and publications from the Department." In addition, it provides links to relevant *Federal Register* documents, press releases, speeches, and legislation.

U.S. National Information Infrastructure Virtual Library. May 29, 1998. Available: http://nii.nist.gov/nii.html (Accessed December 8, 1998).

Connect here to learn more about the information superhighway, how it works, and its ongoing development.

Welcome to the White House. Available: http://www2.whitehouse.gov/WH/Welcome-nt.html (Accessed December 8, 1998).

Options include links to "Commonly Requested Federal Services," "Interactive Citizens' Handbook," and "White House History and Tours." Click on "The Briefing Room" for current federal statistics. Also included is a "White House for Kids."

Yahoo's List. © 1994–98. Available: http://www.yahoo.com/education/ (Accessed December 8, 1998).

Choose from a wide array of education-related links.

Internet/World Wide Web Sites— State and Regional

The following list provides examples from Texas and the Southwest of sites mounted by state or regional agencies and organizations. To discover what is available locally, check the state education agency or association, and the state library and library association.

Department of Information Resources. Available: http://www.dir.state.tx.us (Accessed December 9, 1998).

Provides access to the "Information Resources Management Act" and the "State Strategic Plan for Information Resources," as well as to "Information Resources Standards."

Government Information. December 18, 1996. Available: http://www.tex-share.edu/ LibraryServices/Government.html (Accessed December 9, 1998).

Among the options are "Texas Government," including the Texas State Electronic Library; "U.S. Government"; "Foreign Government"; and "International Agencies."

Southwest Educational Development Laboratory. Available: http://www.sedl.org/ (Accessed December 9, 1998).

Choose from "Content Areas," which includes "Language and Cultural Diversity," "Education Policy," and "Rural Schools"; or click on SEDL to read about other programs.

The Southwestern Bell Science Education Center. Available: http://tiger.coe. missouri.edu/~swbsc/ (Accessed December 9, 1998).

Experiment with "Initiatives in Science Education." Newly added are classroom activities for science teachers.

State of Texas Government Information. November 3, 1998. Available: http://www.texas.gov/ (Accessed December 9, 1998).

Explore traveling, working, and conducting business in Texas; read the Texas Constitution; find useful 1-800 state telephone numbers; and access other useful Texas government information.

WestEd. *Welcome to WestEd.* © 1996, 1997, 1998. Available: http://www.wested.org/ (Accessed December 14, 1998).

Information about and links provided by this organization which "acts as a catalyst and mentor for improving schools." Click on "Our Work" for a list of program areas including assessment and standards development, and educational technology. "Resources" includes information resources.

Media

Ferguson, Jacqueline. *The Grant Organizer: A Streamlined System for Seeking, Winning and Managing Grants.* [diskette and manual]. Alexandria, VA: Capitol Publications, 1993. System requirements: IBM PC; DOS editor knowledge or word processing software capable of converting ASCII text.

Grants and Grantsmanship: How to Design a Successful Grant Application. [video-cassette]. Springfield: Illinois State Library, 1995.

Rife, Patricia. *Grant Writing: A Hands-on Approach.* [2 diskettes and manual]. Haiku, HI: Envision, 1993. System requirements: Macintosh, HyperCard 2.0 or higher, or HyperCard Player to operate.

Case Studies

The literature contains many articles that discuss how grants were obtained and used. The following examples discuss specific grant projects.

Gillespie, Thom. "High-Tech Libraries of Tomorrow—Today." *Library Journal* 116 (February 1991): 46–49.

Harada, Violet H., and Margaret Nakamura. "Information Searching Across the Curriculum: Literacy Skills for the 90s and Beyond [ESEA grant enabled three Hawaii school libraries to expand access to electronic resources]." *Catholic Library World* 65 (October/November/December 1994): 17–19.

"Mother Targets Store for Grant [Chicago seven-year-old's love of books results in various corporate donations to the Sabin School]." *American Libraries* 26 (November 1995): 1002.

Sadowski, Michael. "The Power to Grow: Success Stories from the National Library Power Program." *School Library Journal* 40 (July 1994): 30–35.

B
Frequently
Asked Questions
About Grantsmanship

What is a grant?

TITLE defines the word *grant* as follows:

> [The giving] of funds, as by the federal government to a state, or by a foundation to a writer, scientist, artist, etc., to support a specific program or project.

One frequently funded educator in Texas has equated a grant with "funding your ideas with someone else's money." These funds can be allotted for services (largely related to remuneration of staff), equipment, or facilities, including remodeling as well as the construction of new buildings. Grants may act as the stimulus for ongoing programs, or as a leverage for other contributions. A grant is intended to supplement, rather than supplant, funding already in place; therefore, one might view it as "icing on the cake"—something like a gratuity.

A September 1991 American Library Association news release provides an example of a library grant:

> The Vienna (West Virginia) Public Library received a $5,000 grant from the Bell Atlantic/ALA Family Literacy Project for a program called CAPER (Children and Parents Enjoy Reading). Families with at least one child aged eight or under will participate in a program emphasizing tutoring for parents, training for parents in how to model reading behaviors, reading/activity sessions for children, and library skills sessions for families. Cooperating agencies include Literacy Volunteers of Mid-Ohio Valley, and Wesley United Methodist Church.

Is grant writing really worth the effort?

Before answering this question, ask yourself another one: If money were not an object, what would I do differently in my classroom or library? If a grant could provide the means to make dreams come true—to teach illiterate parents how to read and how to help their children learn, to give at-risk children hope for a future, to provide additional tools and technology for lifetime learners—how could anyone begrudge the time spent applying for a grant?

Nevertheless, one should undertake grant writing only if prepared to invest the appropriate time and effort. If you enter the arena with any illusions in this regard, evaluator comments appended to your first proposal will prove enlightening. One source directed toward librarians provides some reasons why grant writing can most assuredly be a positive endeavor:

> 1. To successfully seek grants you must be able to convincingly state your library's case. Developing your case statement is a healthy exercise requiring enthusiasm and fresh perspective. Every library needs enthusiasm and fresh perspective.
>
> 2. Grantseeking is outreach. It requires that you examine your services from a marketing perspective—from the point of view of the view. For example, you can stop worrying about how to make the community aware of the library, and start making the library aware of the community. Successful proposals are written with the users' benefits in mind.
>
> 3. Raising funds means raising friends. The contacts you make at each stage of the grantseeking process can be new allies for your library. Most funders are not passive dispensers of cash, but partners in projects to improve the quality of life.

4. You have a head start and an advantage. Any book about grants will tell you that research is a major factor in developing successful projects. You are, by training and experience, a research expert.

5. Grantseeking gives you power. When you invest the time to develop a visionary project, you are in control of your library's destiny.

What are my organization's chances of obtaining a grant?

If you follow funders' instructions explicitly, it is entirely possible that you could enjoy a success rate of approximately 50 percent after two or three attempts. When considering a particular grant offering, you might ask the funder to disclose the odds of obtaining a grant. Then consider the following factors concerning the funder:

1. Number of proposals received for the past year.

2. Number of proposals funded for the past year.

3. Average amount per award for the past year.

4. Number of grants being offered this year (if applicable).

5. Total amount of funding available this year.

Is obtaining a grant easier than obtaining funds through other approaches?

Bake sales might be better, or charity bazaars, or raffling donated goods. . . . If given a major emphasis, any approach will probably be more effective than other fundraising options, including grantseeking.

How many grant dollars are awarded annually?

Too many to state an approximate estimate. Within the United States, the total is in the billions of dollars. The Grantsmanship Center, Los Angeles—the largest private organization of grant writers in the nation—can provide fairly accurate statistics. The federal government share of grant dollars, though it has been shrinking for more than a decade, remains large. Schools have been particularly influenced by the School-to-Work Initiative and Tech Prep grants in recent years. In contrast, the corporate sector has been responsible for increasingly larger amounts of grant funding. Grants from foundations and other organizations within the private area, although constituting the smallest part of the total, are also increasing. Not as tradition-bound as the other sectors, private sources offer a more diversified array of possibilities in which grantseekers can develop creative, problem-solving models.

What must I do to obtain a grant?

Submit a grant proposal. For details about how to write a proposal, as well as its structural components, see Chapter 3.

How do I determine who awards grants?

If you have a particular institution in mind, try to establish direct contact. Generally, the closer your liaison with the funding source, the better your chances of ultimately obtaining funding. If you are interested in federal grants, a helpful place to begin is the United States government home page. To learn about grants issued by various state governments, you might begin by contacting either the governor's office or the chief educational official. The Foundation Center (79 Fifth Avenue, New York, NY 10003; 1-800-424-9836) offers the best coverage for anyone interested in private-sector grants. No central compilation currently exists for corporations; however, incomplete listings (often dated as well) are available in a number of reference tools and texts devoted to grantsmanship.

Is it easier to obtain government or private grants?

It depends entirely on what kind of project you want to undertake. If pursuing government grants, you'll be faced with considerably more rules. Be prepared to dot your *i*'s and cross your *t*'s. Both the private and corporate sectors allow for a greater degree of negotiation prior to the submission of the final proposal.

Although government grants typically require more paperwork and have more stringent guidelines than grants from other types of funders, the result may be worth the effort. Federal agencies often offer multimillion dollar grants, whereas private and corporate funders rarely offer awards of more than $1 million. Still, smaller grants may require as much paperwork as larger grants.

What are "foundations"? Will they award grant money to my organization?

According to one source, there are more than 27,000 nonprofit organizations in the United States engaged in awarding grants to other nonprofit organizations to promote the public good. These organizations comprise four basic categories of foundations:

1. **Independent Foundations:** Funds are usually derived from a single source, such as an individual or a family. Some of these foundations are known as "family foundations"; members of the original donor's family serve on the foundation board or staff and provide strong direction for the foundation's funding activities. Others, such as The Ford Foundation or The Rockefeller Foundation, are no longer directed by family members and have broader discretion in executing the funding mission of the original donor. These foundations may focus their grants in a few specific subject areas, or they may award grants for a wide variety of projects. About 70 percent of these foundations limit their grants to a specific local area, usually the state or community where they operate.

2. **Company-Sponsored Foundations:** Legally independent organizations funded by a corporation, these foundations usually have close ties to the corporation providing the funds. Their grants tend to be in fields related to the interests of the corporation or in regions where the corporation operates.

3. **Operating Foundations:** Generally, these foundations manage or operate their own research or service projects, such as a museum or a performance arena, and seldom award grants to other organizations.

4. **Community Foundations:** These foundations derive funds from many individuals and corporations within their local community and award grants to organizations or projects that specifically benefit that community. Most of these foundations operate under slightly different tax laws than private foundations, but their grant programs are similar. Many community foundations are involved with local nonprofit organizations, providing management assistance and advice on fundraising in addition to their grant programs.

Prior to applying for a foundation grant, it will be necessary to obtain information about the following:

1. The foundations that are willing to support agencies in your region for the type of project you are proposing.

2. The size and type of grants these foundations are willing to award.

3. The steps to take in applying for grant support. Because each foundation has different grant interests and limitations, as well as different application procedures and deadlines, your success in acquiring a grant will largely depend on your knowledge of the funder.

How do I determine what a funding agency really wants in a proposal?

Ask the funding agency. Funders don't want you to fail in your quest for grant money. However, they are often overwhelmed by applications and don't want to waste valuable time sifting through undeserving proposals. Adhere closely to submission guidelines. Funder logic is as follows: If an applicant doesn't follow proposal rules, the applicant probably won't adhere to established guidelines in implementing and executing the grant-funded project.

Furthermore, think of funders and proposal evaluators as synonymous. One seasoned proposal evaluator has offered the following tip:

> Before I even check to see if a proposal is in accordance with established guidelines, I take in several things. I look for a font size that doesn't cause eyestrain, for plenty of white space and approximately one-inch margins. I notice the aesthetic appearance of the proposal. I like to see bits of color, some relief from pages and pages of narration; for example, graphics, charts, pictures. A proposal that is too "busy," meaning too many different fonts or visually crowded space, is a real turnoff. And all of this occurs within thirty seconds from the time I pick up the proposal, before I've even started reading it.

Must I know the "right people" to obtain a grant?

It never hurts. Private- and corporate-sector agencies are generally organized to channel you directly to key personnel. However, government bureaucracies are designed to overcome any inherent advantages a particular grantseeker might have with regard to prior contacts. Despite the official slant, though, a close relationship with important government officials (or their friends and associates) probably helps in the acquisition of grants.

How much grant money should I request?

Be prudent: Ask for only what you really need. Do not include requests for money to supplement insufficient local funds. It may also be tempting to insert into the budget purchases of services, equipment, and items you want to acquire that are essentially superfluous to executing the project. A skilled proposal evaluator will detect this practice. It could ultimately result in denial of funding.

How can I spend grant money?

You can purchase almost anything you want—insofar as it contributes to addressing the target population's need as expressed in the proposal. The current trend within all funding sectors has been to modify guidelines so that grantseekers can explore creative options.

How difficult will it be to obtain my first grant?

Very difficult. Fortunately, if you apply yourself, it becomes easier with repeated efforts. Improvement is most likely to occur through

1. making contact with the funder;

2. cultivating collaborative efforts within the grant development team;

3. networking with experts in the fields related to your project.

Can I obtain a grant to cover regular operating expenses?

Rarely, if ever. Commonly referred to as "operations and maintenance" costs, these expenses are frequently covered by "friends" of the organization in cases when normal budgetary channels prove insufficient. Grantseeking is typically reserved for finding the resources to develop new projects, or to extend existing projects that have considerable potential.

How many pages is a typical proposal?

There is a wide range of variation in the length of this document. The expectations of the funder are the primary factor in determining length. Some proposals— particularly those that essentially are a response letter or a completed application form—are as short as one page. Government agencies, most notably at the federal level, set very precise limits for length (e.g., 20 pages of standard text; or 50 pages overall, including appended materials). Grant proposals seeking large sums of money and not limited to length can sometimes contain hundreds of pages.

How specific must the proposal be?

The degree of proposal specificity depends on funder requirements. Don't try to overwhelm the funder with superfluous detail. However, you can never know too many specifics about what you want to accomplish through your project. Funders know that the ultimate success of the project depends upon thorough research.

Can I request grant money for indirect as well as direct costs?

Indirect costs appear in the project budget as expenses incurred by the grant recipient in executing a project that are not clearly related to the direct expenditure of funds for goods and services. They are nevertheless vital to the successful execution of a project. Examples of indirect costs include maintaining facilities, providing administration, and depreciation. This is money that the grant recipient doesn't account for when budgeting execution of the project.

The flexibility you have in requesting funds for such costs varies considerably from one funding agency to another. In some cases, the funder provides explicit guidelines. For example, the Texas Education Agency establishes a specific percentage rate (of the total project allotment) for indirect costs in its grants to specific school districts. The rate varies slightly from district to district (e.g., Aldine Independent School District was allowed a maximum of 2.5 percent of the total project allotment for indirect costs). Indirect costs are often determined through a series of negotiations between the funder and chief financial officer of the grantseeking organization. This official submits the agreed-upon limits to the grant development team during the proposal writing stage.

Should I talk with the funder before submitting a proposal?

Yes—whenever possible. Funders have information that they didn't supply in the request for proposal (RFP). The formality of the grant announcement process doesn't allow the funder to provide all the information you'll want to know. An added benefit of speaking directly with the funder: You will be remembered during the proposal evaluation process. Attendance at a proposal conference can also be helpful by allowing you exposure to the questions asked by other grantseekers. A Texas school district grants officer remembered a recent visit to the Department of Education (DOE) in Washington, D.C., in which she asked a DOE program director, "Can you give me any tips or hints of things you like to see—or don't like to see—in a proposal?" Her page of notes regarding the director's response contained entirely new information compared to the DOE's request for application.

Can I obtain copies of successful grant proposals?

In many cases, absolutely. Government funders are legally required to provide copies of previously submitted proposals on request. However, they will often request that you query them in writing. Private and corporate funders, though, frequently have a policy of not making proposals available to the public, for a variety of reasons.

Obtaining copies of proposals in this manner is generally worth the effort because they can prove to be very instructive. Remember, though, that each new project is bound to include unique features. Even the replication of an earlier project will result in a modified proposal because of factors such as 1) different institutions involved, 2) different target groups, 3) an altered time frame, and 4) the acquisition of previously generated findings. Therefore, the perusal of old proposals should serve only as a rudimentary initiation to writing a new proposal and grant development team activities. Remember, funders are looking for innovative projects, not recycled projects they funded during previous years.

How long does it take to write a proposal?

The writing process, from beginning to end, is not a short-term endeavor. The less experience you have with the process, the less time you are likely to spend. As grant writers gain more experience, they typically devote increasing amounts of time and energy to the task. The authors estimate an average of approximately 100 hours for each proposal writing effort.

How should I organize the proposal?

The funder will usually direct how you structure the proposal. It is important that you follow these instructions explicitly. If the funder asks that only particular information be included, you might employ a standard format such as the one set forth in Chapter 3. Contact the funder first regarding any possible guidelines (e.g., length of the overall proposal).

How successful in obtaining grants are other organizations like mine?

You'll always think they are more successful than you are. In reality, the success of any organization in obtaining grants depends on its efforts, beginning at the top of the administrative hierarchy. If you request it, the funder will usually share specific data about grant awards from previous years.

How do I obtain early access to information about new grant opportunities?

Currently, maintaining a competitive edge necessitates searching the Internet daily. Most funding agencies provide information by this means. Commercial online vendors such as DIALOG (Knight-Ridder) and BRS (Maxwell) require payment of user fees, but they offer comprehensive databases devoted exclusively to the availability of grants. E-mail and word-of-mouth communication can be extremely useful in requesting information from a particular funding agency. However, subscription to relevant journals, newsletters, and other print resources is still helpful for keeping abreast of emerging grant opportunities. (See "Tools for Discovering Funding Sources" in Appendix A for a list of print and Internet/World Wide Web resources.)

Why would anyone want to award a grant to my organization?

There are many reasons. You may be able to help further the funding agency's mission or enhance its prestige. Every funder is part of a local community; funders often view themselves as partners in improving the schools, public libraries, and cultural contributions in the area. When a funder awards a grant, this act gives its personnel a sense of fulfillment; awarding grants allows them to help make the world a better place.

Nevertheless, remember that every funder has an agenda. You can't expect something for nothing. Your success depends on understanding the funder's objectives, and then selling to the agency the services you can offer. Your proposal should convince the funder that the needs of your target population will remain neglected unless the funder helps. A well-written needs statement (see Chapter 3) will indicate to the funder that a compelling need exists and must be addressed.

How can I enlist help from other people in planning and writing a proposal?

Simply ask them. Most competent staff are willing to help others because they received needed assistance at some time. Individuals are most inclined to help when you

1. are not directly competing with them for grant funds;

2. schedule sessions involving them well in advance;

3. work within planned parameters and avoid unanticipated requests;

4. don't ask them to do something outside their area of expertise (e.g., don't ask an accountant to provide a rough draft of the budget section of a proposal if he or she isn't experienced and comfortable writing such material);

5. incorporate them into the project (e.g., a college professor asked to serve as an external evaluator will likely offer to help write the evaluation plan).

Whom should my organization designate as the project director?

The first impulse is often to recruit the highest-ranking person within the organization. However, this person is not always the best choice. Typically, the person who knows the most about the proposed project is the individual most qualified for the job. This individual is more likely to possess the vision necessary to manage the project successfully. The project director must be easy to contact by telephone. It is frequently necessary for the grantor and the grantee to negotiate funding or to discuss program activities. A teacher or librarian working with a room full of students cannot abruptly leave to answer a telephone call. Likewise, individuals who travel frequently are not consistently easy to contact.

Does hiring a professional grant writer enhance my organization's chances of receiving funding?

Absolutely not. Someone outside the organization rarely can ascertain the needs of the target population, the skills and strengths of employees, and other internally specific factors. Employing a professional grant writer can therefore diminish the organization's chances of acquiring a particular grant. A Texas Education Agency staff member was overheard stating the following about grant applicants:

> We can spot a central office-generated proposal in a minute. We want to hear from people on the front lines. A central office administrator can't know the students' learning styles or individual needs, or even a given school's surrounding neighborhood.

However, many grant development teams might benefit from employing a professional writer to review and edit the proposal prior to submission. Such experts can be especially effective if they spend time on-site, closely collaborating with the team.

What reference tools should I use in developing a proposal?

Begin by assembling as many publications delineating your organization and its mission as possible. Obtain resources documenting institutional funding (when such information is accessible and not classified). Consult the indexes, abstracts, and bibliographies likely to include references to research relevant to your project. Librarians excel at surveying and locating available literature, and are thus indispensable members of any grant development team.

How can I avoid the last-minute rush in submitting the proposal?

The issuing date for most grants is cyclical. Once you have determined the general timeline for a funder's cycle, it will be possible to complete much of the writing well before the submission deadline (even in cases when the official announcement of a deadline leaves little turnaround time). The grant development team's response time to deadlines can be shortened by maintaining ongoing files concerning their organization, including résumés of key staff, annual reports, mission statement, composition of the board of directors, and historical background of the organization (including previous grant awards), as well as community demographics and other documents and information that will likely be necessary.

Is grantsmanship really worth all this effort?

Sometimes the decisions made by your organization's administrators leave you no choice but to become involved in the grant development process. For example, public colleges and universities have faced a steady decline in state funding; they have had to prioritize grantsmanship as a means of supplementing their operating budgets. Schools are also experiencing the pressure to aggressively seek grant funds. In some cases, the push to involve staff in grant development is not worth the time required for training, planning, proposal writing, and so on. Many staff don't respond well to this new and stressful development, particularly when job performance ratings and merit raises are contingent upon their involvement and achievement in this process. Some staff simply don't have the particular capacity necessary to excel at grantsmanship. More important, these individuals—as well as those who have talent for grantsmanship—are being divorced from the very tasks they were initially hired to do (teaching, supervising existing programs, etc.). At the very least, staff who are heavily involved with grant development should be relieved of some of their original duties by equally capable replacements.

Above all, organizations must acknowledge that grantsmanship isn't for everyone. Staff should be allowed the option to remain outside the process without being made to feel that they have less value to the organization.

C
Glossary

Terms Related to the Grantseeking Process

Abstract

A summary description of a proposed project. Usually no more than one page in length, it concisely states the main points of the proposal, including the rationale, objectives, and proposed methods of research and evaluation.

Accountability

The responsibility of the grantee to thoroughly account for and report disbursement of grant money as well as to relate the disbursement of money to the results of the funded project. An audit is sometimes part of this process. The increasing awareness of the extent of human needs in contrast to the limited financial resources available to meet them has led funders to increasingly emphasize accountability.

Action grant

A specific type of grant awarded to support action research.

Action research

Exploration of a situation or service that occurs as part of the regular activity within the organization conducting the research. Action research attempts to resolve a local problem or provide a local service. This immediate, specific application distinguishes action research from theoretical research. *See also* Applied research *and* Theoretical research.

Applicant

The individual, group, or organization seeking a grant. Upon being awarded a grant, the applicant becomes known as the grantee.

Application for supplement

The process of asking a funder for additional money beyond what has already been granted for a particular project. If granted, these funds are known as a supplement or supplemental grant. Typically, the same terms, conditions, and time limits stipulated in the original grant also apply to the supplement.

Application kit/package

A package of materials supplied by the funding agency that generally includes instructions and forms required for submitting a grant application. Sometimes called a request for application (RFA).

Application notice

An announcement that a funding agency is accepting applications for a particular grant. The notice may include a brief description of the scope and amount of the grant along with contact information and the application deadline. Funders often post notices in professional-association publications or in government sources such as the *Federal Register.*

Applied research

Research primarily concerned with solving a specific human problem. Applied research thus differs from theoretical research. *See also* Action research *and* Theoretical research.

Approval/disapproval time

The amount of time taken by a funder to review—and decide—which applications merit monetary support.

Assurance of compliance

Documentation assuring the funder that the grant applicant acts in accordance with regulations governing such areas as Affirmative Action, rights of human subjects, humane treatment of animals, and appropriate certification of personnel. Assurance of compliance is particularly important when applying for government grants.

Authorization

Legislation authorizing the implementation of a government grants program.

Begging/stealing

Terms used by some grantseekers to describe their actions to obtain grant money from funders, whom they perceive as naive, ignorant, or inclined toward feeling pity for grantseekers. This abstract image of funders unfairly "giving away" or haughtily "bequeathing" money can negatively influence grantseekers' interactions with funders and their success in obtaining funding. *See also* Vanity funding.

Behavioral objectives

A statement of anticipated project outcomes that concern the changing of actions of the target population. They should be measurable both before and after project execution. *See also* Broad, long-term objectives *and* Specific objectives.

Bid list

A compilation of potential respondents to a request for proposal (RFP), or a compilation of grant applicants. Those listed may benefit by receiving early notification of funding opportunities.

Biographical sketches

Background information about the key project personnel often required by a funder as part of the application kit/package. This data generally includes education, research and professional experience, honors/awards, memberships in relevant committees and associations, and publications.

Block grant

A category of federal grant dispersed within broad subject areas. Limited control is delegated to local or regional authorities.

Boilerplate

A section of any document, particularly a grant proposal, that has been used so frequently that it has become a standardized feature, undergoing little, if any, modification with each application.

Broad, long-term objectives

The ultimate goals of the project proposed in a grant application. Usually not achievable within one particular cycle of the project, they reflect what the principal investigator (PI) is attempting to accomplish during the life of the project. In contrast, specific objectives are generally achievements within one cycle of the project. *See also* Behavioral objectives *and* Specific objectives.

Budget

The portion of a proposal detailing estimates of project income and expenditures for a given length of time. Brief descriptions of project functions and anticipated outcomes related to the financial data may be included as part of the budget. *See also* Budget justification *and* Multipocketed budgeting.

Budget justification

The portion of the grant application that provides a rationale for the funds itemized in the budget. It is sometimes referred to as the budget detail or line-item budget.

Categorical grant

A governmental grant (usually at the federal level) issued under specific program guidelines that delineate, in detail, considerations such as eligibility requirements, program time frames, and intended beneficiaries.

CFDA number

A unique number that the compilers of the *Catalog of Federal Domestic Assistance* assign to each federal program listed in this source.

Challenge grant

More commonly referred to as a matching grant, a challenge grant is offered by a funder with the stipulation that the prospective grantseeking organization enlist another funder to share a portion (usually ranging from 10 to 50 percent) of project costs. Federal grant programs use this provision to ensure the participation of local resources in grant programs.

Channeling

The process whereby a tax-exempt and more credible and visible intermediary organization accepts funds from a grantor and passes them directly to a predesignated grantee.

Client

The person or group designated as the recipient of the services provided by the grant-supported project. The group of clients are also known as the target population.

Conceiver

The person credited with the original idea for a grant project. This individual focuses the project and can be instrumental in interpreting it to the funder, project staff, clients, and other participants.

Conceiver's disease

A term used to describe a continuous generation of ideas for grant-supported projects.

Conceptual dexterity

Skill in expressing ideas in terms that the audience (e.g., funders, program participants, other proposal planners) can relate to and understand.

Consortium

Two or more groups allied contractually for a particular project or common mission. Normally, funders will require documented assurance that all members of the consortium will comply with all applicable laws and policies.

Contingency funding

Support offered with the provision that the grantee comply with specified requirements (e.g., Equal Opportunity mandates).

CON (contract opportunity notice)

A public announcement indicating an organization's interest in obtaining a particular type of service. Less specific in describing the service sought and project requirements than a request for proposal (RFP), a CON is used primarily to determine the most qualified applicants.

Contract

A type of grant award facilitating the procurement of research. The funding agency typically requires greater accountability from the recipient regarding project requirements than for noncontract grants.

Cost benefit

A method of evaluating a product or service by comparing the expense of acquiring and maintaining it against its utility.

Cost sharing

The division of expenses among organizations that will derive benefits from the project. In some cases, grantors give preferential status to proposals that involve cost sharing.

Data collection procedures

The process, generally determined prior to the outset of a project, concerned with gathering statistics, survey results, and other data as a basis for evaluating the project's effectiveness and efficiency.

Data sharing

Detailed examination of test results, survey responses, or other information gathered in preparation for—or as part of—a grant-funded project. Various statistical methods and statistical analysis software are typically used in the data analysis process.

Defunding

An expression used to describe a decision by project auditors to postpone or withhold the release of grant funds.

Demonstration grant

Funds awarded to support a project that is in some way innovative or unique. These projects serve as models for others to emulate; therefore, they involve publicity of all types, including arranging site visits, compiling reports, writing articles, presenting papers, and videotaping project activities. Money is awarded to demonstrate or prove that the particular project succeeds in achieving its stated objectives and goals.

Direct costs

Expenditures specifically associated with the execution of a project, including employee compensation, travel, equipment, supplies, and costs relating to publications ensuing from the project. Anticipated expenditures are submitted as part of the grant application and, as such, must be approved by the funding agency. *See also* Indirect costs.

Discretionary funds

Money that a project administrator can allocate as deemed appropriate. These funds are a nonbudgeted award allocated without categorical designation as to how they are to be spent.

Discretionary grant

A grant that allows the funder to decide the type of project to support (e.g., a project for research, training, etc.) as well as the level of support (e.g., 50 percent of costs, start-up costs only, etc.).

Dissemination

The process of communicating and distributing information related to funded projects. It may involve reports, press releases, articles in newsletters or journals, conference presentations, videotapes, student portfolios, service directories, and so on.

Documentation

The records containing the data related to a project, including the budget, staff communication, minutes, survey results, observation reports, client dossiers, student academic achievement, and so on. This material provides the basis for evaluating the project.

"Doing your homework"

An expression used to describe the process of learning as much as possible about a funder before applying for a grant. Relevant activities include basic research in libraries, studying the publications of the funding agency (e.g., annual reports, newsletters), and networking with previous grant recipients. The determination of a detailed cost breakdown of materials, supplies, and services related to the project is also part of this process.

Donor

An individual, group, or organization who contributes money, products, or services for a project.

Donor control

The amount of power or influence that a donor can exert over the disposition of the grant award. Some experts argue that donors should have little control because they are inclined to indulge their biases; a committee comprised of community representatives is more likely to understand community needs. However, those favoring donor control believe that many donors are predisposed to risk funds on genuinely innovative grant projects.

Effectiveness

A measurement of the effects or results of a grant project. To gauge effectiveness, the grant proposal should include a description of desired outcomes as well as the method employed for measuring the effectiveness of project outcomes.

Efficiency

The relationship between the amount of effort expended and achieved results. An efficient project seeks to eliminate unnecessary or duplicate processes.

Endowment

Donated funds that are invested, rather than spent, by the recipient. Income from the investment is used to award grants, defray operating costs, pay taxes, and so on.

Evaluation

Measuring the degree to which program objectives have been achieved. Though the process tended to be executed rather informally in the past, recent years have seen the application of more rigorous qualitative and quantitative techniques in upgrading funding, service delivery, project management techniques, and so on. *See also* Formative/process evaluation *and* Summative/product evaluation.

Exemplary project

A project distinguished by the funding agency as one that sets a standard for grantseekers in the same field to emulate in designing project proposals. An exemplary project differs from a demonstration project; the former focuses on process, whereas the latter focuses on a unique or innovative element within the project.

Expenditure responsibility

The funder's legal liability (e.g., Tax Reform Act of 1969) for assuring that all grant funds are used strictly for philanthropic—not personal or political—purposes. The law stipulates that recipients of grants either possess tax-exempt status or be capable of qualifying for it if they were to apply. If these conditions are not met, the funding agency is responsible for determining that each expenditure has an appropriate philanthropic, religious, or educational purpose. Because of limited staff resources, many private foundations have entered into contractual arrangements with community foundations whereby the latter assume responsibility for funding groups lacking a tax exemption. *See also* Channeling.

Expository writing

A type of narrative writing intended to formally clarify or explain a topic. It is usually employed in writing grant applications and proposals, scholarly articles, and so on.

Formative/process evaluation

An analysis of whether the methods and techniques employed in a project achieved outcomes as intended. *See also* Evaluation *and* Summative/product evaluation.

Formula grant

A financial award based on interpretation of a predetermined set of criteria (e.g., number of rural schools within a given district, percentage of libraries lacking Internet access). Essentially the opposite of a competitive grant, a formula grant requires applicants to document that their project meets eligibility conditions. Revenue sharing is a type of formula grant at the federal level.

Foundation

An organization established for charitable purposes. It generally incorporates 1) an endowment—provided by a donor—which is invested to generate an income to distribute as grants, and 2) a committee that determines who will receive funding. Types of foundations include public (i.e., community foundations) and private (which can be further subdivided into general-purpose, special-purpose, family, and operating foundations).

Funder

An individual, group, or organization who sponsors or awards grant money (or both). The major types of funders include government, foundations, and business/corporate.

Funding cycle

The recurring grant process that includes the announcement of funding opportunities, proposal review, and grantee notification. The application deadline typically defines the structure of a funding cycle. These cycles may be scheduled at set intervals, or funders may remain continuously involved with the various stages of the grant process.

Funding period

The amount of time covered by the allotment of grant funds. The period is generally one year, although the grant provision also may include a renewal option.

Gantt chart

A method—developed by Henri Gantt—for sequentially displaying the relationship between tasks and the time required to accomplish them. A Gantt chart is particularly useful for planning and tracking a project.

Giving pattern

A profile of the projects previously funded by a particular agency; the amount of the grant allotments; the location of the funders; and the types of organizations conceptualizing, sponsoring, and managing the projects. This data provides the basis for assessing a particular applicant's chances of being awarded a grant.

Goal

The broad-based development that the grant is intended to facilitate. In contrast, an objective focuses on more specific portions of the project, documenting desired modifications in terms of the size of the target population, the level of activity or skill, and deadlines.

Grant

An allotment of money or other resources (e.g., services, etc.) by a funder with the intent of facilitating the project delineated in the grantee's proposal. A grant differs from a contract in that 1) the funder does not receive any economic dividends from the allocation; 2) it is philanthropic in nature—it either alleviates dependency or increases cultural opportunities; and 3) the grantee renders the transaction possible and defines the parameters by which grant funds may be expended.

Grantee

An individual, group, or organization that has been awarded a grant by a funding agency.

Grants-in-aid

Another term for grant.

Grantsmanship

The ability to locate and obtain grant funding. Some experts have noted that this term is often used negatively, implying that grants tend to be awarded based on the ability of the applicant to manipulate the funder rather than on merit. *See also* Begging/stealing.

Grants officer

The government agency representative directly responsible for administering a grant program. This person is usually the most vital contact during both the proposal preparation and the grant funding periods.

Grantspeople

Any persons responsible for the grantseeking process, including researching funding agencies, managing preparation of proposals, analyzing relevant service-delivery systems, providing mediation among project participants, and recruiting additional personnel to execute project activities. Also known as grantseekers.

Grievance procedure

The process by which applicants whose proposals were not funded can appeal that decision. Grievances range from requests to obtain further information about why the proposal was declined, to presenting documentation that the grant was awarded to a less qualified applicant.

Guidelines

The funder's stated goals, priorities, eligibility criteria, and application procedures. Generally, guidelines either equip the applicant for the proposal writing process or incorporate forms that, when completed, comprise the proposal itself.

Hard match

Monetary funds. *See also* Soft match.

Hard money

Dependable, long-term funding sources that most likely originate from either government or large fundraising agencies (e.g., the United Way). Changes in priorities, inflation, tax cuts, and so on, sometimes cause hard sources to turn soft (*see* Soft money).

Human services

Programs that provide various types of assistance to people (e.g., homeless shelters, day care), as opposed to services supporting research, purchases of equipment or facilities, and so on.

Indirect costs

A category of grant funding often provided by funders to assist in defraying grantee operation expenditures that are typically shared with other projects (e.g., administrative functions; maintenance of physical facilities such as cafeterias, utilities, parking facilities, libraries, and rest rooms; etc.). The grantee and the funder negotiate funds for indirect costs, which are typically calculated using a percentage formula based on total direct costs. Generally, the grantee is not required to specify how funds for indirect costs will be spent. *See also* Direct costs.

Information overload

An inability to focus on the most important information when confronting more data than the senses can efficiently assimilate. Inexperienced grant writers often face this problem.

In-kind

The applicant's contribution to the proposed project. This can include materials (e.g., supplies, equipment), office space, services (e.g., free Internet access), and so on.

Intervention

Action taken to keep a problem from becoming worse. Intervention is sometimes the impetus for the grant project.

Investigator

See Principal investigator (PI).

Joint funding

A funding situation in which multiple funders each contribute either to a specified portion/activity or to a common monetary pool for the grant project. A notable Texas grants coordinator coined the phrase "village initiative" to describe this situation.

Laundering federal money

The process of realigning the priorities of a federal funding program for closer compliance with state or local priorities.

Letter of commitment (to the project)

A letter indicating exactly what resources the grant recipient will commit to the project if funded.

Letter of inquiry

Correspondence required by some funders before the applicant is sent instructions regarding the submission of a formal proposal. In some cases, funding agencies require specific inclusions in this letter.

Letter of intent

A statement, sometimes required by grantseeking institutions, indicating that the principal investigator (PI) plans to apply for a specified amount of money from a particular funder within a particular time frame. The letter enables the organization to decide whether it is 1) committed to—and capable of—complying with grant specifications if funded, and 2) opposed to applying for a grant that fails to include overhead costs and would, therefore, severely tax institutional resources. It also informs the funder how many evaluators will be required for reviewing the proposals.

Letter of support

Project endorsements—appended to a proposal—contributed by persons and organizations that the funder will likely consider sources of expert assurance.

Leveraging

Also known as dominoing and pyramiding, this is the use of one grant to obtain another.

Mainstreaming

The reintegration of any group traditionally set apart from society. In the past, it had a narrower meaning: the process of shifting special-education students into the regular classroom.

Mandate

A funding agency's mission, or the problem that it is attempting to solve. Sometimes agencies make grants available as a means of achieving their goals.

Matching

Obtaining additional funds from sources outside the funding agency. Federal government and foundation grant programs often dictate that applicants obtain a portion of the funding—typically 10 to 50 percent of total project costs—from other sources. The strategy for the applicant is to establish the presence of strong local support for a particular proposal.

Multipocketed budgeting

The process of securing funding from a variety of sources, each of which may either provide assistance for a particular project component or unrestricted finances to be disbursed as needed.

Narrative

The explanatory section of a proposal. Typically, in federal government grant programs, it enlarges upon the application form.

Needs assessment

An attempt to convince the funder that a particular project is desirable or necessary. It is often augmented by means of surveys or questionnaires, the findings of which can provide the basis for a grant request.

Overhead deficit

The deficit when comparing the amount of funding for overhead costs received for a project to the overhead costs needed to actually support the project. In cases where an overhead deficit exists, the grantseeking institution needs to withdraw from the application process. If committed to the project, the institution has a number of options, most notably either taking the funds from its endowment or raising the funds from private donors, investment income, fees obtained from commercial grantors, and so forth.

Packaging

Communicating the essentials of a proposal by effectively addressing the specific priorities, objectives, and guidelines of various funders.

Payout requirement

The legal mandate directing private foundations in the United States to annually offer grants based on the larger of two amounts: net investment return versus 6 percent of the total investment value.

Peer review

The process by which a proposal is assessed by experts culled from the field it addresses.

Preliminary reviewers

Experts responsible for examining and appraising—in written form—the relative merits of grant applications.

Preliminary studies

The section of a grant application documenting the principal investigator's (PI) survey of prior work undertaken and data accumulated that underscore the validity of the proposed methodology. These studies can assist in relating the experience and capabilities of an investigator to the execution of the proposed project.

Pre-proposal

Also known as a preliminary proposal, discussion paper, or preapplication, this is a concise proposal format employed by some funders to determine which projects are most deserving of consideration in a final screening for grant awards.

Primary reviewer's reports

An evaluation of a grant application addressing the import—from scientific, technical, and other perspectives—of the proposed research; originality; strength of the methodology; qualifications, experience, and potential of the principal investigator (PI) and staff; appropriateness of the proposed resources, facilities, and services; adaptability of the budget; suitability of the requested time frame; and additional considerations such as assurances and certifications.

Principal investigator (PI)

The individual (often the person whose idea initiated the project) charged with chief responsibility for a proposed project. This individual is responsible for executing the activities delineated in the grant application, communicating with the funder, writing continuation applications, and so on. Also known as the primary investigator.

Pro bono publico

A Latin phrase ("for the public good") referring to people or organizations who volunteer time and professional services to charitable causes (e.g., legal counseling, medical screening, consulting). A means of obtaining services and expertise not otherwise available because of limited funding.

Proposal

The document submitted when applying for a grant. Its prime functions include describing, selling, planning, contracting, and evaluating. Types range from an informal letter or simple application form to explicitly detailed projections of proposed research. Typical sections include a cover letter, identification pages, abstract, table of contents, introduction, survey of the literature, needs assessment, goals and objectives, methodology, activities statement, budget, personnel description, evaluation design, future funding plans, dissemination of findings, and letters of support.

Public sector

The entities given tax dollars for supplying designated public services. Within the grants sector, it includes federal, state, and local government, as well as community foundations and some tax-exempt organizations.

Research design

A description of the project methodology to be used to achieve stated objectives.

Revenue sharing

A type of formula grant program administered by the Department of the Treasury beginning in 1972. It enabled money derived from personal income taxes to be distributed to local jurisdictions on a discretionary basis, within broad limits.

RFA (request for application)

A formal notice denoting a funder concern along with an invitation to experts within the specified field to submit grant applications.

RFP (request for proposal)

An announcement provided by a funder interested in obtaining a service from a contractor. Federal government RFPs tend to be extremely elaborate, delineating the activities, qualifications, and so on, deemed necessary by the funder.

Risk capital

A portion of profits designated to the exploration of risky options. Public-service entities so disposed tend to rely on infusions of grant funding.

Sacrifice trap

The inclination of some grantors to fund the same applicants repeatedly in an attempt to rationalize initial outlays.

Seed grant

A small monetary allotment made by a funder to motivate a potentially worthwhile organization or project.

Service delivery system

The infrastructure of an organization involved with the concerns addressed by its own proposal. Because funders are disinclined to award grants for a duplication of services, it is imperative to ascertain that the planned project complements or enhances prior efforts.

Set-aside

Grant money designated for particular persons or organizations in advance of the application process. Often ensuing from lobbying efforts, this practice lessens the competitive aspect of grantsmanship.

Sign-off

The signing of documents, by a sponsor's authorized representative, that will enable the applicant to obtain funder support.

Site visit

A funder's direct look at an applicant's organization. A site visit may occur as early as the application stage, or as late as the evaluation stage, near the end of the grant-funded period.

Soft match

Non-monetary awards (e.g., services, facilities, equipment, etc.).

Soft money

Short-term funding generally available for no longer than 12 months.

Specific objectives

Goals to be achieved within one cycle of the project. In a grant application, they typically take the form of brief notation, sometimes using an outline format. They can include behavioral objectives, research intents, or hypotheses to be tested. *See also* Broad, long-term objectives *and* Behavioral objectives.

Spinoff disease

Diverting time and energy from an existing project to the development of extensions and variations of its basic plan. *See also* Spinoff projects.

Spinoff projects

New projects developed to address previously unrecognized needs that have become apparent through execution of the original grant project. Spinoff projects are often subsidized using funds obtained through the initial grant proposal. *See also* Spinoff disease.

Sponsor

Sometimes known as a fiscal agent, this entity supplies the grant recipient with credibility, services, space, and so on—anything but money.

Subcontract

A contract between the grant applicant and other persons or groups for acquiring resources and services necessary to achieve project goals.

Summative/product evaluation

An analysis of project outcomes.

Support services

Activities (e.g., clerical and maintenance operations) that facilitate the accomplishment of an organization's primary functions.

Target population

The projected beneficiaries of a grant-funded project. A member of the target population is also known as a client.

Technical assistance

Information and training assistance offered to grant applicants by funders (e.g., dissemination of applicable regulations, involvement in proposal writing, recruitment of promising grant candidates). Services from a particular funder can be instrumental in obtaining a grant from another source.

Technical review

Critical evaluation of a proposal by experts culled from the discipline addressed by the applicant's project.

Theoretical research

Research concerned with expanding knowledge or making a contribution to the theory or body of knowledge within a particular discipline. *See also* Action research *and* Applied research.

Topic sentence

The first sentence of a paragraph; it indicates the information to be discussed in that paragraph. Given the expository writing style used in grant proposals, effective topic sentences can help evaluators, who are required to scan many long documents, decide which paragraphs to initially skip while still focusing on essential information. The topic sentences in transitional or continuation paragraphs may not need to be so explicit.

Unexpended funds

Grant money not yet spent as the designated time frame of the project nears completion. The increasing pressure to disburse these funds prior to the beginning of a new funding cycle may lead to an "11th-hour" giveaway.

Unrestricted funds

Grants that are awarded without previously established conditions for expenditure.

Unsolicited applications

Funding programs not dictated by firm application deadlines. Few government agencies accept unsolicited applications; however, most foundations and corporate funders do.

Vanity funding

Funding ensuing from a grantor's desire for ego gratification as opposed to altruism or a commitment to a particular type of grant project. *See also* Begging/stealing.

Terms Related to Automation and Telecommunications Technology

A significant portion of the grant proposals currently being submitted by schools and public libraries are concerned with the need to upgrade technology for education and information dissemination. The resources required include computers, modems, facsimile machines, VCRs, instructional and reference software (e.g., CD-ROMs), access to commercial online services and the Internet, voice-only teleconferencing, and interactive two-way video. Also needed is training for teachers and librarians to effectively use technology as a tool for enhancing learning and access to information.

An understanding of the following terms and concepts is vital to preparing successful grant proposals within the realm of technology. Most technical terms and concepts referenced in passing have their own entries, including unexpanded acronyms and abbreviations.

Analog gateway

A means of connecting dissimilar codecs to allow analog-to-digital (and vice versa) communication. An analog gateway allows for interoperability in a nonstandard environment (an environment using both analog and digital signals), but can be plagued by problems such as a degradation of audio/video reception and reduced functioning of the technology.

Analog transmission

A continuous transmission expressed by bandwidth, or range of frequencies. Broadcast television, cable television, and AM/FM radio are transmitted on analog channels. *See also* Digital transmission.

AppleTalk

Apple Computer's proprietary LAN for linking Macintosh computers and peripherals. As of 1997, the network ran at 115Kbps and would accommodate up to 32 devices.

ASCII

American Standard Code of Information Interchange, a code for representing alphanumeric information.

Audioconferencing

Also known as audio teleconferencing, it is a form of voice-only communication linking people at two or more sites by standard telephone lines. Speakerphones are used to allow several people to participate at each site; an audio bridge is often used to link three or more sites.

Audiographics conferencing

Point-to-point computer and voice conferencing whereby two people connect computers and telephones to collaborate over an onscreen document. The collaborative file is shared between the computers and user controls are displayed on each individual computer. The telephone connection does not necessarily employ the same network as the computer connection.

Audio subcarrier

The frequency transmitting audio for direct-broadcast purposes (e.g., radio) or to complement a video signal (which is carried on a different frequency).

Bandwidth

The number of electrical frequencies a device can handle. For a network, the higher the bandwidth, the greater the amount of data that can be passed through it, and the higher its quality. One video channel—the equivalent of 1,200 voice telephone channels—requires a relatively high-capacity (high-bandwidth) data circuit.

BIOS (basic input/output system)

The portion of the disk operating system (DOS) in each workstation that performs the actual communications with input and output devices, such as printers, drives, keyboards, and consoles.

Bit

A binary digit, the basic signaling unit used in all digital transmission.

BNC

A bayonet-locking connector for slim coaxial cables, such as cables used with Ethernet. BNCs are also used with high-quality video cables and to network interface cards, transceivers, and other interactive devices.

Bridge

A device that 1) links three or more locations to facilitate multipoint video- or audioconferencing, or 2) connects two or more networks and sends packets of data between them.

Bulletin board service

A service enabling remote users to access a central "host" computer to read and post electronic messages.

Carriers

Vendors of transmission services that provide local, long distance, or value-added services. As proprietors of a communications medium, they rent, lease, or sell portions at a price set by tariff to the public through shared circuits.

CATV (community antenna television)

A method of delivering quality television reception by taking signals from a high antenna favorably situated within the community and delivering them to people's homes through a coaxial cable network. The electrical components of such systems are also used to create broadband LANs. The key components are the "head-end," which originates all the signals; the cable, which delivers the cable and the switching; and amplifying components, which perpetuate the signals to their destinations.

CCITT

Acronym for International Telephone and Telegraph Consultative Telecommunications Standards Committee.

Chair person control

In setting up a multipoint videoconference, one of the sites may request chair person control of audio/video transmission. This site generally builds the conference parameters of the MCU, thereby determining on/off status for the 1) "request the floor" feature, and 2) voice-activated switching feature.

Channel

An electronic path for transmission between two points. Also referred to as a circuit, line, or link.

Chip

A thin silicone wafer on which electronic components are deposited in the form of integrated circuits. It is the basis of all digital systems.

Classroom facilitator

The primary communication link between the instructor and the distance learning coordinator through the application of skills in program planning, technologies, and troubleshooting.

Client/server model

Refers to an architecture for LAN applications programs in which the software is divided into client and server components. Running on different machines, the server component provides data for the client component, whereas the client component interacts with the user. The most common example is a database server. This is a database management system (DBMS) with functions split into a "front-end" that interacts with the client to enter data, ask questions of the data, and write reports, and a "back-end" that stores the data, controls access to data, protects data, and makes necessary changes to the data. The primary advantages of the client/server model are 1) less network traffic, 2) much better performance, and 3) greater flexibility in the application and availability of data.

Cluster

A group of educational institutions located within a defined geographic area and directly interconnected by video channels.

Coaxial cable

A vinyl-insulated cable consisting of a central conducting copper wire insulated within another cylindrical conducting wire. It can carry considerable quantities of data, including video.

Codec (coder-decoder)

A device that encodes and decodes analog signals into digital signals and vice versa (e.g., in videoconferencing, codecs code and decode video and audio signals).

Compression

Reduction of the amount of information content to accommodate cost-effective digital transmission. For example, video information can be compressed by either reducing the quality by sending fewer frames per second or by transmitting only the changes that occur from one frame to the next.

Computer conferencing

The process by which people at different locations communicate directly with each other through computers, usually in real time. New applications are generically known as whiteboarding (two-way annotation on a white screen) (*see* Electronic whiteboard) and application sharing (both users make changes to the other's document or spreadsheet).

Continuous presence

MCUs with the capability of displaying up to four sites on a monitor at each of the sites by electronically splitting the outgoing signals.

CONUS

Acronym for Contiguous United States.

CPE

Acronym for Customer Precise Equipment.

DCS or DACS (digital cross-connect switch)

An electronic switch located in a telephone company central office that can reroute channels on request. In IETV applications, it may be used to interconnect various clusters without the need for many channels.

Digital

Information contained in the form of 0s and 1s for transmission on digital media, including fiber, microwave, and satellite. Such information may include video, audio, graphics, and data.

Digital switch

A device facilitating multiway conferencing in a fully digital network, generally with voice-activated switching.

Digital transmission

Whereas an analog signal is a continuous wave, digital transmission is a code of discrete binary signals (e.g., on and off, 0 and 1, high and low). It is expressed by a rate of data flow in bits per second. *See also* Analog transmission.

Distance learning

Any form of electronic information access over space, including the Internet, online database searching, electronic "field trips," and multimedia.

Downlink

A satellite dish and associated electronic devices and components that receive signals from a satellite.

Dual 56

A combination of two lines transmitting at 56Kbps to create a video transmission capacity of 112Kbps. The most frequent application permits direct dialing of a videoconference call.

Echo chamber

An electronic device that eliminates echo or feedback in audio transmissions.

Electronic whiteboard

A means by which graphics can be shared simultaneously among two or more computers over a telephone network. Each user is able to view and annotate the graphics as desired.

Encryption

The alteration of transmitted information to protect it from unauthorized tapping.

Ethernet

> A 10Mbps network using either coaxial or twisted-pair cable developed at Xerox's Palo Alto Research Center. DEC and Intel have cooperated with Xerox to make Ethernet a network standard that provides computers with LAN access on a transmit-at-will basis (i.e., when two transmissions collide, they wait and try again until they transmit successfully).

Facilitator

> The individual responsible for the local component of a videoconferencing site.

FAX (facsimile) machine

> A telecopying device that electronically transmits written or graphic material over telephone lines to produce a hard copy at a remote location.

FDDI (fiber-distributed data interface)

> Refers to an ANSI standard for a 100Mbps fiber optic LAN that uses a "counter-rotating" token ring topology.

Fiber optics

> A communication medium based on a laser transmission employing a glass fiber that carries light to transmit video, audio, or data signals. Each fiber can carry digital information at a rate of 90 to 150Mbps, or 1,000 voice channels.

Frame

> From a video perspective, a frame is a single picture displayed on a television monitor. It consists of two interlaced fields of 525 lines (the current NTSC standard) transmitted at the rate of 30 frames per second. In videoconferencing, a variable number of frames per second are sent, depending upon the bandwidth available. (Typically, from 8 to 30 frames per second are sent. Motion in video looks "jerky" when transmitted in fewer than 12 frames per second.) *See also* PAL.

Frames per second

> The frequency at which video frames appear on a monitor. Broadcast-quality video is widely considered to have a frequency of 30 frames per second, whereas full-motion videoconferencing is generally considered to have a frequency between 10 and 15 frames per second. The rate is sometimes lower at very low bandwidths.

Full-duplex audio

> Audio transmission that enables users at remote sites to speak simultaneously without losing audio contact. It can be employed in a point-to-point or multipoint conference. *See also* Half-duplex audio.

Fully interactive audio/video

Interaction between two or more videoconferencing sites by means of audio and video signals. It is possible for sites to be fully interactive without necessarily having full-motion capability.

GHz (gigahertz)

1,000MHz, or 1 billion hertz (Hz).

Graphics

Transmission of still images, usually from a video source (a camera or presentation stand), but in some cases PC-generated. Graphics may also include onscreen annotation involving drawing or text.

Graphics camera

A camera located within a teaching room that is dedicated to photographing written or pictorial representation. It can be ceiling-located to focus on a desktop, or directed toward a whiteboard (*see* Electronic whiteboard) or wall. *See also* Pan/tilt camera.

Half-duplex audio

Audio transmission that allows speaking from only one site at a time. *See also* Full-duplex audio.

HDLC (high-level data link control)

An international standard communications protocol developed by the International Standards Organization.

HDTV (high-definition television)

Video reception that includes more than 1,000 lines of resolution (standards vary from country to country) and employs the 16x9 screen-ratio format. (Regular TV consists of 525 lines and a 4x5 format.)

H.221

The International Telecommunication Union-Telecommunication (ITU-T) sector standard relating to the communications protocol for videoconferencing.

H.243

ITU-T recommendation setting the procedures for establishing communication between three or more videoconferencing sites.

H.261

ITU-T codec communications protocol for audio and video. Specifies the video and audio coding algorithms that make it possible for video codecs from different manufacturers to communicate successfully.

H.320

The family of ITU-T videoconferencing standards that enable dissimilar systems to communicate with each other.

Hz (hertz)

The basic measure of frequency with which an electromagnetic wave completes a full cycle from its positive to its negative pole and back again. It is a unit of frequency equal to one cycle per second.

In-band

Transmission occurring within the allocated bandwidth (e.g., a video call with a total of 384Kbps could allocate 32Kbps for audio, leaving 352Kbps for video).

Interactive

Communication in which all participating sites have equal capability (e.g., audio/video reception and transmission).

Interoperability

A state of complete compatibility among devices required to operate together.

ISDN (integrated services digital network)

Consists of two basic forms: BRI (basic rate interface) and PRI (primary rate interface). BRI is also referred to a 2B+D because it supplies two bearer channels of 64Kbps each and one data or signal channel of 16Kbps. PRI is also know as 23B+D because it provides 23 64Kbps channels and one 16Kbps data channel (the total of 1.544Mbps equals a *T-1* line).

ITU-T

The International Telecommunication Union-Telecommunication sector was established by the United Nations and includes membership from the governing agencies of most national governments. It is primarily concerned with setting telecommunications standards.

JPEG (joint photographic experts group)

Refers to a video compression standard for storage and transmission of compressed still and video images relating to multimedia.

Kbps (kilobits per second)

1,000 bits per second. A measure of the rate of digital transmission.

kHz (kilohertz)

1,000 hertz (Hz).

LAN (local area network)
> A short-distance data communications network (typically restricted to a building or campus) employed to link together computers and peripheral devices under some form of standard control.

Mbps (megabits per second)
> 1 million bits per second. A measure of the rate of digital transmission.

MCU (multipoint control unit)
> This device facilitates switching and conferencing video calls among three or more videoconferencing locations, all of which are employing the same data bandwidth.

Mediaconferencing
> The ability to conduct a complete information exchange across distance, including video, audio, document, computerized-data, and time conferencing.

Mhz (megahertz)
> 1,000 kHz, or 1 million hertz (Hz).

Modem
> A device that converts digital computer signals into analog format for transmission.

MPEG (motion picture experts group)
> A motion video and audio compression standard. Originally used on a widespread basis for the storage and playback of multimedia images from CD-ROM format, it has been increasingly applied to broadcasting and videoconferencing.

Multiplexer
> A device that facilitates the subdivision of a given bandwidth (e.g., a *T-1* multiplexer may divide a T-1 transmission line [with a capacity of 1.544Mbps] into two capacities of 768Kbps each).

Multiplexing
> Allows for the simultaneous transmission of two or more information streams over a single physical medium. The most widely used forms include FDM (frequency division multiplexing), TDM (time division multiplexing), and WDM (wave division multiplexing), which applies to transmission using fiber optics.

Multiway
> Communication among more than two sites occurring through either a digital switch or an analog gateway.

Network

Two or more information sources or destinations (also referred to as points or nodes) linked by communications media to exchange information.

NIC (network interface card)

A device that enables a computer to communicate with other workstations or fileservers.

NTSC

Acronym for North American National Television System Committee. Refers to a 525-line standard for a frame of color TV.

Out-of-band

Transmission that occurs external to allocated bandwidth (e.g., video calls with out-of-band audio require a separate phone line for the audio).

PAL (phase alternate line)

Refers to the European standard of 625 lines per frame, 25 frames per second with respect to analog video.

Pan/tilt camera

A camera equipped with gears and braking to facilitate a full circular range of motion, generally remotely controlled. *See also* Graphics camera.

Px64

The ITU-T's international video standard based on a specified algorithm for video compression and decompression. Adopted in December 1990, it is also known as H.261.

Point-to-point

Communications between two locations.

Point-to-multipoint

Communications from one location to several locations.

POP (point of presence)

Designates the point at which responsibility for handling inter-lata traffic is assumed by the inter-exchange carrier.

Rate-adapted videoconferencing

Originally conducted using an analog gateway, this form of videoconferencing has been adapted to a modified MCU employing a digital switch known as a Multiway Conferencing System (MCS). It enables multiple sites to conference with one another simultaneously at different transmission speeds.

"Request the chair"

In a multipoint videoconference, one of the sites can send a request signal to the site with chair person control. The chair site will then decide whether or not to give control to the requesting site.

Requirements survey

The systematic study of a building (or group of buildings) to determine the needs for voice and data telecommunication equipment and distribution data.

Resolution

A measure of sharpness or clarity on a video monitor.

RGB (red, green, blue)

Represents the three separate pictures employed in color video systems. They are merged together as a composite signal for normal video. For maximum picture quality and in computer applications, however, the signals are separated.

Router

An interface that determines the best route between any two networks, even in cases where there are intermediate networks.

RS-232

Codec connectivity (interface) permitting data inputs for transmission from .3 to 19.2Kbps.

RS-449

The transmission interface between the codec and the transmission link that typically connects to a T-1 multiplexer.

Satellite

A device put into orbit to receive and transmit signals as an intermediate link between terminals on Earth.

Satellite uplink equipment

A satellite dish that transmits signals to a satellite.

Site licensing

A method of licensing software for use by everyone at a particular site for a single fixed fee (as opposed to requiring that each user have a license for their individual copy of the software).

Slow scan

The use of transmitters that scan selected frames and transmit the visual information over telephone lines to receiving sites, where it is reconstituted as a still picture. Also refers to still-frame video that accepts an image from a camera or other video source one line at a time.

T-1 (DS-1)

A digital transmission link with a capacity of 1.544Mbps. Constructed of two pairs of normal twisted phone wires, T-1 lines connect voice and data networks across long distances. LANs are interconnected over T-1 networks (i.e., WANs) by means of bridges or routers.

T-3 (DS-3)

A digital transmission link with a capacity of 45Mbps. A T-3 channel can carry 28 T-1 channels. T-3 channels are used for digital video transmissions or for major PBX-PBX interconnection.

T-120

A group of ITU-T standards instituted in 1996 (e.g., transmission of graphics to multiple sites during multipoint videoconferencing).

Telecommuting

The process of "commuting" to work electronically rather than physically.

Teleconferencing

Any conferencing system using telecommunications links to connect remote sites. There are many types of teleconferencing, including videoconferencing, computer conferencing, and audioconferencing.

10Base-T

The Ethernet LAN works in homeruns in which the twisted-pair wiring from each workstation is connected directly to a 10Base-T hub. This network possesses two notable advantages: 1) if one workstation crashes, it doesn't crash the entire network, and 2) the network is easier to manage because the 10Base-T hubs are controlled by sophisticated management software.

Token ring

A ring type of LAN in which a supervisory frame or signal, known as a token, must be received by one workstation before it can begin transmitting using the network's entire bandwidth. The LAN always works logically as a circle, with the token passing around the circle from one workstation to another at a transmission rate of either 4 or 16Mbps.

Twisted-pair cable

A cable composed of two small insulated conductors twisted together. Differential noise is minimal because both wires are equally exposed to any interference.

UTP (unshielded twisted-pair wiring)

A cable medium with one or more pairs of twisted insulated copper conductors bound in a single sheath. It remains the most common method of bringing telephone and data to the desktop.

Video mixing

An MCU feature that allows users at each site to simultaneously view one or more sites other than the site viewing them.

Videophone

A telephone combined with a video screen allowing callers to see each other as they speak.

Voice-activated multipoint videoconferencing

A situation in which the MCU is set to switch among sites depending on who is speaking.

WAN (wide area network)

The interconnection of LANs over T-1 networks using bridges or routers.

Index

Abstract, 49, 50, 63, 127
Accountability, 127
   guarantee of, 81
Accountants, 72
Achilles, Charles M., 102
Acronyms
   use of undefined, 95
Action grant, 127
Action Guide to Government Grants, Loans and Giveaways, The: A Home Study Course (Chelekis), 103
Action research, 127. *See also* Applied research; Theoretical research
Action verbs
   in goal statements, 28
   in project narrative, 61
   and project objectives, 31
Administrative support
   importance of, 6
Administrators
   on grant development team, 1
   and pre-development planning process, 9
   and technology initiative activities, 41
Advisors, 86
Advisory committee/group, 41, 42, 91
Affirmative action, 128
African-American groups
   library services to, 27
Age Discrimination Act of 1975, 69
Agreement
   proposal function as, 48
Ally, Brian, 107
Alstete, Jeffrey W., 38
"Alternate Funding Sources: Corporate Funding: Finding New Partners" (Goldberg), 108
America Goes Back to School
   web site, 110

American Association of School Administrators
   web site, 111
American Association of School Librarians
   web site, 105, 111
American Library Association, 116
American Standard Code of Information Interchange. *See* ASCII
Americans with Disabilities Act, 69
Analog gateway, 143
Analog transmission, 143
Announcements
   obtaining, 9
Annual Register of Grant Support, 102
Appendices, 49, 59–60
   components of, 59–60
   in submission to funding source, 64
Apple Computer, 143
Apple Partners in Education
   web site, 105
Apple Support Information
   web site, 111
AppleTalk, 143
Applicant, 128
Application for supplement, 128
Application kit/package, 128
Application notice, 128
Applied research, 128. *See also* Action research; Theoretical research
Applied Research Center
   web site, 111
Approval/disapproval time, 128
ARC–Applied Research Center
   web site, 111
Ariel font, 97
Art of Writing Successful R&D Proposals, The (Orlich and Orlich), 28
Articles
   for dissemination, 57

ASCII, 144
Assessment team, 82, 83
Assurance of compliance, 128
Audio subcarrier, 144
Audioconferencing, 144
Audiographics conferencing, 144
Audiovisual materials
    for dissemination, 57
Audit, 127
Authorization, 128
Automation and technology terms,
    143–55
Averages
    in descriptive statistics, 84
Award
    negotiating nature/extent of, 2
Award notification
    timeline for, 87

Background data
    for proposal development process, 7
Bandwidth, 144
Bauer, David G., 60, 102
Bayley, Linda, 107
Begging/stealing, 129. See also Vanity
    funding
Behavior modification, 37
Behavioral objectives, 129. See also
    Broad, long-term objectives;
    Specific objectives
Belcher, Jane C., 94, 102
Bell Atlantic/ALA Family Literacy Project,
    116
Benchmarking in Higher Education:
    Adapting Best Practices to Improve
    Quality, 38
Benefits
    for target group, 23
Bequests
    for continuance funds, 59
Bernhard, Elizabeth A., 102
"Best practices," 42
    for proposal development process, 7
Best Practices in Education
    web site, 111
"Best practices" sites, 1
    travel to, 6
    visits to, 38–39
Bibliographic databases
    access to, 7
Bibliography, 59
Bid list, 129
Big Book of Library Grant Money, The,
    102

Biographical sketches, 129
BIOS (basic input/output system), 144
Bit, 144
Block grant, 129
"Blue ribbon" sites, 42
BNC, 144
Boilerplate, 129
"Book Business, The: The Bookstore as
    an Alternative Funding Source for
    the Public Library" (Sumerford),
    110
Books/manuals
    for dissemination, 57
Brainstorming, 20
Branch libraries
    promotion of flexibility of, 44
Brewer, Ernest W., 102
BRI (basic rate interface), 150
Bridge, 144
Broad, long-term objectives, 129. See also
    Behavioral objectives; Specific
    objectives
BRS (Maxwell)
    grant opportunity information via, 123
Budget, 49, 55, 129. See also Budget
    development; Multipocketed
    budgeting
    adjustments and amendments to, 78
    funder detection of padded, 95, 97
    personnel, 66
    in submission to funding source, 64
Budget detail, 55
Budget development, ix, 71–79
    additional budgeting considerations,
        77–79
    preparation of budget, 72–76
    role of budget, 71
    types of budgets, 71–72
Budget formatting
    influence of funding agencies on, 77
Budget justification, 76, 130
Budget summary, 55
Bulletin board service, 145
Bullets
    and proposal design, 61
Business and industry leaders
    on grant development team, 1
Business community
    involvement of, 98
Business partners
    importance of collaboration with, 86
"Business-School Partnerships: Future
    Media Center Funding Sources"
    (Sumerford), 110

Calendar, 92. *See also* Project calendar
  adjusting
Campus improvement plans
  strategies for, 42–43
CAPER (Children and Parents Enjoy
  Reading), 116
Capital campaigns
  for continuance funds, 59
"Careful Planning: The Fundraising Edge"
  (Sumerford), 110
Carlson, Mim, 52, 53, 55, 84, 103, 107
Carriers, 145
Case studies, 35, 36, 114
Cash match breakdown, 77
Catalog of Federal Domestic Assistance,
  103, 130
Categorical grant, 130
CATV. *See* Community antenna television
Cause-and-effect relationships, 84
CCITT (International Telephone and
  Telegraph Consultative
  Telecommunications Standards
  Committee), 145
CD-ROMs, 143
Certifications
  for project personnel, 68
CFDA number, 130
Chairperson
  control, 145
  selecting, 15
Challenge grant, x, 130
Change(s)
  cautious approach to, 79
  commitment/mandate for, 8
Channel, 145
Channeling, 130
Charts, 97
  and project design, 54
  in project narrative, 62, 120
Chelekis, George, 103
Childcare center library programs, 27
Children
  and parental involvement, 44
Chip, 145
Chi-squares
  in inferential statistics, 84
Civil Rights Act of 1964, 69
Clarity of purpose
  failure to convey, 95, 97
Classroom facilitator, 145
Client, 130
Client/server model, 145
Cluster, 146
Coaxial cable, 146
Codec (coder-decoder), 146

Cohesive effort
  problems from lack of, 25
  and project design, 37
Collaboration
  breakdown of, 26
  laying foundation for, 37
  and organizational capability, 35
Colleagues
  discussions among, 38
College professors
  as external evaluators, 85
Color
  in project narrative, 62, 120
Commercial online services
  access to, 143
Communication
  effective, 14, 15
  importance of during project, 92
Communications, 72
Community antenna television (CATV),
  145
Community diversity
  in project advisory group, 42
Community foundations, 119
Community Information Referral Centers,
  27
Community mandates
  matching to funders, 30
Community participation/perspective,
  44, 98
  for campus improvement plans, 43
  and project design, 21
Company-sponsored foundations, 119
Compatibility
  between funder and organization, 15
Competition
  factors in, 21
Competitive grant. *See* Formula grant
*Complete Grants Sourcebook for Higher
  Education, The* (Bauer),
  60, 102
Comprehensive proposal, 46, 49
Compression, 146
Computer conferencing, 146
Computers, 143
CON. *See* Contract opportunity notice
Conceiver, 130
Conceiver's disease, 130
Concept paper
  proposal function as, 48
Conceptual design of project
  meetings about, 17
  methodologies for, 35–37
  preliminary checklists for, 33
  steps in, 20–24 (table 1-7)

Conceptual dexterity, 130
Conference grant, x
Conferences
    for dissemination, 57
Congressional representatives
    letters of support from, 90
Consensus
    within Working Group, 43
Consensus building
    and project design, 25
Consortium, 131
Construction grant, x
Consultant contracts
    drafting, 92
Consultant services, 55
Consultants, 5, 75
Consulting grant, x
Contingency funding, 131
Contingency management, 37
Continuance funds
    applications for, 2
    identifying best sources for, 59
    sources for, 58–59
Continuing education
    and professional development, 39
    and technology initiative activities, 41
Continuous presence, 146
Contract, 131
Contract negotiations, 78–79
Contract opportunity notice (CON), 131
Contract services, 55
CONUS (Contiguous United States), 146
Cooperating institutions council, 41
Coordinator of grants development/
        management
    on grant development team, 1
Copying, 72
Corporate 500: Directory of Corporate
        Philanthropy, 103
Corporate funders
    and budget formatting, 77
Corporate sector grants, 117
Corporations, 4
Cost benefit, 131
Cost sharing, 131
Costs/financial resources
    for grant development process, 6
"Count on Reading," 111
Courier font, 97
Cover letter, 60
    in submission to funding source, 63
Cover sheet, 49–50
    in submission to funding source, 63
CPE (Customer Precise Equipment), 146

"Creating a Fundable Monster" (Norris),
        109
Credibility, 50, 51
    and subcontracts, 79
Criticism
    dealing with, 91
Cultural differences
    sensitivity to, 23
Cultural diversity
    and professional development, 40
Currency
    of information for proposal development
        process, 7
Curriculum development, 35
Curriculum-related projects, 36
Curriculum specialists
    on grant development team, 1

Data collection methods/procedures,
        83–84, 131
    identifying, 24
Data sharing, 131
Dates
    in proposal development calendar, 11
Deadlines, 2
    and calendar development, 10
    failure in meeting of, 95, 96
    proposal submission, 88
    for team members, 14
DEC, 148
Defunding, 131
Delegating, 14
Demonstration grant, x, 132
Dental insurance, 75
Department of Information Resources
    web site, 113
Descriptive statistics, 84
Design
    evaluation, 81
    of proposal, 61–62
    and proposal writing, organization
        guidelines, 60–64
Designing Successful Grant Proposals
        (Orlich), 110
Detail
    lack of attention to, 95, 96
Development officer, 4
DIALOG (Knight–Ridder), 7
    grant opportunity information via, 123
Digital, 147
Digital cross-connect switch (DCS or
        DACS), 147
Digital switch, 147
Digital transmission, 147

Direct costs, 132. *See also* Indirect costs
    grant money for, 122
Directory of Research Grants, 103
Disadvantaged persons
    library services to, 27
Discretionary funds, 132
Discretionary grant, 132
Displays
    for dissemination, 57
Dissemination, 132
    of findings, results, products, 49, 57–58
    grant, x
    in submission to funding source, 64
Distance learning, ix, 147
Document issues
    and proposal preparation, 19
Documentation, 132
DOE professional development guidelines,
    39
"Doing your homework," 132
Dominoing, 138
Donor, 133
Donor control, 133
Downlink, 147
Drafting timetable
    adherence to, 48
Drug abuse prevention programs, 27
Drummond, Tom, 111
Dual 56, 147
Dumochel, Robert, 103

Echo chamber, 147
Editing. *See also* Writing
    proposal, 18–19, 125
Editor
    selecting, 19
Educate America Act: Goals 2000, 44
*Education Grantwinners: Models of Effec-
    tive Proposal Structure and Style*
    (Ratzlaff), 110
Educational degrees
    for project personnel, 68
Educational institutions
    disbursement of funds through, 98
Educators
    as evaluators, 85
*Effective Evaluation: A Systematic Ap-
    proach for Grantseekers and Project
    Managers*, 107
*Effective Grant Office, The: Streamlining
    Grants Development and Manage-
    ment*, 108
Effectiveness, 133
Efficiency, 133

Electronic databases
    potential funder information in, 9
Electronic Learning
    web site, 106
Electronic whiteboard, 147
E-mail, 14
Employee benefits, 75
Employment compliances, 69–70
Encryption, 147
Endowment, x, 133
Equipment, x, 55, 70, 72, 92
Equitable access mandate, 40, 43
ERIC (Education Resources Information
    Center)
    web site, 112
Ethernet, 148
Ethics
    of solutions, 23
Evaluated design
    proposal function as, 48
Evaluation, 133. *See also* Formative/
    process evaluation; Summative/
    product evaluation
Evaluation criteria
    and project objectives, 30
Evaluation design, 81
    guidelines for, 56
    and research implications, 49, 55–57
    in submission to funding source, 64
Evaluation methods
    formative evaluation, 81, 82–83
    summative evaluation, 81, 83
Evaluation process
    importance of, 55
    overview of, 81
Evaluation reports, 81
Evaluation teams, 84–86
Evaluators, 86
    external, 85
    internal, 55
    meetings with, 91
    responsibilities of, 55, 57
    selecting, 84
Executive summaries
    for dissemination, 58
Exemplary project, 133
Expected outcomes
    in submission to funding source, 64
Expenditure responsibility, 134. *See also*
    Channeling
Expenses. *See also* Budget
    estimating, 24
Experimental studies, 35
    pitfalls associated with, 36–37
    vs. surveys, 36

Expository writing, 134
External evaluation, 55
　teams for, 85–86

Facilitator, 148
　selecting, 15
Faculty members
　on grant development team, 1
Failed proposals, 94–98
Family foundations, 119
FAX (facsimile) machine, 143, 148
FDDI (fiber-distributed data interface),
　148
FDM. *See* Frequency division multiplexing
Feder, Jody, 102
Federal Express
　pickup/delivery schedules for, 13
Federal funding
　decline in, 4
Federal government
　and project adoption curriculum
　　grants, 36
　share of grant dollars awarded by, 117
Federal grant funding agencies
　hiring funds through, 66
Federal grants
　timeline for, 87
Federal programs officer, 4
Federal Register, 103, 128
　web site, 105
Ferguson, Jacqueline, 108, 114
Ferrell, Edith H., 108
Fiber optics, 148
FICA, 55
Financial resources, 6–7
*Finding Funding, Grantwriting and Project
　Management from Start to Finish*
　(Brewer, Achilles, and Fuhriman),
　102
Flextime, 5
Fonts
　and proposal design, 61, 120
　unappealing, 95, 97
Food and Nutrition Information Center
　web site, 112
Ford Foundation, 119
Formative evaluation, 48, 55, 81, 82–83
Formative/process evaluation, 134
Formative program evaluation, 2
Formatting issues
　importance of, 19
Formula budgets, 71, 72
Formula grant, 134
Foundation Center, The, 118

Foundation Center, The
　web site, 105
*Foundation Center's Guide to Proposal
　Writing, The* (Geever), 108
*Foundation Center's User-Friendly
　Guide: A Grantseeker's Guide
　to Resources*, 108
Foundation Directory, 103
　annual updates through DIALOG,
　　107
Foundation grants
　pre-application information gathering
　　for, 119
Foundation Grants Index, 104
　quarterly updates through DIALOG,
　　107
Foundations, 4, 134
　categories of, 118–19
　grants from, 117
Frame, 148
Frames per second, 148
Frequency distributions
　in descriptive statistics, 84
Frequency division multiplexing (FDM),
　151
Friends groups
　disbursement of funds through, 98
"Friends of the Library Book Sales"
　(Sumerford), 110
Fringe benefits, 55, 72
*From Idea to Funded Project: Grant Pro-
　posals That Work* (Belcher and
　Jacobsen), 102
Frost, Gordon Jay, 108
FTE. *See* Full-time equivalent
Fuhriman, Jay R., 102
Full-duplex audio, 148. *See also* Half-
　duplex audio
Full-text databases
　access to, 7
Full-time equivalent (FTE), 74, 75
Fully interactive audio/video, 149
Functional and program budget
　(combined)
　example program budget for, 73
　　(table 5-1)
Funder perspective
　and project design, 22
Funder(s), xi, 134
　partnerships with, 89
　proposal format specifications by,
　　49
　reasons for grant awarding by, 124
　talking with, 122
　thank-you letters to, 90

Funder's guidelines
  and abstract, 50
  failure in following, 95, 96
  grantseeker compliance with, 47
Funding agencies/sources
  aligning organizational mission with, 15
  appropriateness of, 10
  discovering, 123
  identifying, 9
  matching proposal to fit interests of, 45
  post-project development, 88
  project objectives and proposal rejection by, 31–32
  researching, 1
  role in proposal writing, 120
  researching, 45
  seeking other, 98
Funding cycle, 134
Funding limitations
  and "best practices" site visits, 38
Funding officers, 89
Funding period, 135
"Fund-Raising and Grantsmanship for the 1990's" (Phillips), 110
Future spending plan, 58
  in submission to funding source, 64

Gantt, Henri, 135
Gantt chart, 135
Garamond font, 97
Geever, Jane C., 108
General purpose grant, x
Geographic balance
  and fund disbursement, 98
Gershowitz, Michael, 108
Get Funded! A Practical Guide for Scholars Seeking Research Support from Business (Schumacher), 104
"Get Going with Grants" (Kaye), 109
Getting a Grant in the 1990s: How to Write Successful Grant Proposals (Lefferts), 104
Getting Funded: A Complete Guide to Proposal Writing (Hall), 104
GHz (gigahertz), 149
"Gifts, Grants and Strings [Hidden Costs of Fund Raising]" (Ally), 107
Gillespie, Thom, 114
Giving pattern, 135
Goal development. See Project goal development

"Goal-Objectives-Activities: How to Translate the Grant Writing Mantra into Fundable English" (Norris), 109
Goal statements
  action verbs used in, 28
Goals and objectives, 49, 63, 135
  within proposal, 52–53
Goals 2000 and Title I: How Two Programs Interact, 108
Goldberg, Israel A., 109
Goldberg, Susan, 108
Gothberg, Helen M., 108
Governance structure
  designing, 41
Government agencies, 4
  and budget formatting, 77
  length of proposals to, 121
Government Assistance Almanac, 103
Government compliances
  observance of, 70
Government grant cycles
  and evaluation team utilization, 85
Government grants
  vs. private grants, 118
Government Information
  web site, 113
Government spending
  reductions in, 29
Graduate courses, 39
Grammar
  errors in, 95, 97
Grant agreement
  signing, 91
Grant announcement process, 122
Grant awards
  management of, 4
  negative result of failing to plan for receipt of, 89
Grant development process
  and administrative support, 6
  flowchart on, 3
  planning, 1–24
  stages in, ix
Grant development team
  documentation available to, 5
  organizational barriers to, 4
  preparation for project design by, 37–38
  responsibilities of, 37
  strengths/weaknesses in proposal reviewed by, 94
  tasks for, 1
Grant dollars
  annual awards of, 117–118

Grant funds/funding
  disbursement of, 92
  strategies for organizations failing re-
      ceiving of, 94–98
"Grant Me This: How to Write a Winning
      Grant Proposal" (Bayley), 107
Grant money
  amounts to request, 120
  spending, 121
Grant opportunities
  access to information on, 123
Grant Organizer, The: A Streamlined Sys-
      tem for Seeking, Winning and Man-
      aging Grants (Ferguson), 114
Grant project
  preparations for successful implemen-
      tation of, 93 (table 7-1)
Grant proposal(s), 118
  obtaining copies of successful, 122
  project objectives at core of, 30
Grant publications/reports
  review of, 39
Grant recipients
  strategies for successful, 89–92
Grant-related consulting businesses, 85
Grant Seeker's Desk Reference (Quick),
      110
Grant Seeker's Directory (Quick), 104
Grant Seekers Guide (Shellow and Stella),
      105
Grant Seeking Fundamentals Workshop
      Workbooks (New and Quick), 109
Grant writers, 4
  pros/cons on employment of, 125
  time and effort expended by, 123
Grant Writing: A Hands-on Approach
      [diskettes/manual], 114
Grant Writing for Teachers: If You Can
      Write a Lesson Plan, You Can Write
      a Grant (Karges-Bone), 109
Grantee, 128, 135
Grant(s)
  chances of obtaining, 117
  determining who awards, 118
  difficulties in obtaining, 121
  reasons for awarding of, 124
  types of, x–xi
Grants
  monthly updates through DIALOG, 107
"Grants: Bonus or Bother?," 108
Grants administrator, 4
Grants and Awards for Teachers, 104
Grants and Grantsmanship: How to De-
      sign a Successful Grant Application
      [videocassette], 114

Grants Central Station
  web site, 105
Grants coordinator
  and negotiation process, 90
Grants Development Kit, 108
Grants Management Kit, 108
Grants office
  proposal scores obtained by, 88
Grants officer, 136
Grantsmanship, poor, 95–98 (table 7-2)
Grantseekers, 45
Grantseeker's Answer Book, The (Fergu-
      son and Gershowitz), 108
Grantseeker's Guide to Project Evalua-
      tions, 108
Grantseeking
  ease of ?, 117
  favorable climate for, 4–5
  impetus for, ix
  success of, xiii
Grants-in-aid, 135
Grantsmanship, xiii, 135
  worth the effort?, 126
Grantsmanship: A Primer for School
      Librarians (Olson), 109
Grantsmanship Center, The
  web site, 106
Grantsmanship Center, The (Los Angeles),
      117
Grantspeople, 136
Grantwriting. See also Proposal; Writing
  worth the effort?, 116–17
Graphics, 149
Graphics camera, 149. See also Pan/tilt
      camera
Graphs, 97
  and project design, 54
  in project narrative, 62, 120
Greivance procedure, 136
Growth, 6
Guide to Funding Databases & Resources
      Online, 108
Guide to U.S. Foundations, 104
Guidelines, 136
Guidelines for Preparing Proposals
      (Meador), 109

Hale, Phale D., Jr., 108
Half-duplex audio, 149
Hall, Mary S., 104
Harada, Violet H., 114
Hard match, 136. See also Soft match
Hard money, 136
HDLC (high-level data link control), 149

HDTV (high-definition television), 149
Headings/subheadings
    in project narrative, 62
Health insurance, 55, 75
"High-Tech Libraries of Tomorrow—
        Today" (Gillespie), 114
Hiring
    formalizing by director, 92
    grant-funded personnel, 91
Hiring and employment compliances,
        69–70
Holden, Carolyn, 108
Holiday delays
    in development calendar, 13
*How To" Grants Manual, The: Successful
        Grantseeking Techniques for Ob-
        taining Public and Private Grants*
        (Bauer), 102
How to Win More Grants, 108
Human services, 136
Hz (hertz), 150

"ICONnect," 111
Ideas
    documenting, 13
Illustrations
    in project narrative, 62, 120
Implementation procedures, 23
In-band, 150
Independent foundations, 119
Independent study, 39
Indirect costs, 136. *See also* Direct costs
    grant money for, 122
Inferential statistics, 84
Infinitive phrases
    in construction of project objectives, 31
Information
    for proposal development process, 7
Information overload, 137
"Information Searching Across the
        Curriculum: Literacy Skills for the
        90s and Beyond" (Harada and
        Nakamura), 114
In-kind, 68, 137
In-kind contributions, 77
In-kind match breakdown, 77
In-kind personnel budget, 78 (table 5-4)
"Instruction in Developing Grant Propos-
        als: A Librarian-Faculty Partner-
        ship [Teaching Students How to
        Apply for Grant Funding and Write
        Proposals]," 109
Integrity
    maintaining, 79

Intel, 148
Interactive, 150
Interactive two-way video, 143
Intergenerational library programs, 27
Internal evaluation, 55
Internal evaluation teams, 85
International Telecommunication Union-
        Telecommunication (ITU-T), 150
    standards of
        H.221, 149
        H.243, 149
        H.261, 149
        H.320, 150
Internet, 43
    access to, 143
    for discussions among colleagues, 38
    funding sources sites on, 105–7
    grant opportunity information via, 123
    and professional development, 39
    project support tools, 110–12
    resources available on, 7
    state and regional sites, 113
Interoperability, 150
Intervention, 137
Interviewing
    project staff candidates, 91
Introduction, 49
    to proposal, 50–51
    in submission to funding source, 63
Investigator. *See* Principal investigator
IRS tax exemption 501(c)(3), 46
ISDN (integrated services digital network),
        150
ITU-T. *See* International Telecommunica-
        tion Union-Telecommunication

Jacobsen, Julia M., 94, 102
Jargon
    overuse of, 95, 97
Job performance ratings, 126
Joint funding, 137
Joint writing committee, 18
JPEG (joint photographic experts group),
        150

Karges-Bone, Linda, 109
Kaye, R., 109
Kbps (kilobits per second), 150
Key dates
    in proposal development calendar, 11
kHz (kilohertz), 150
Kollasch, Matthew, 109
Kussrow, Paul G., 109

LAN. *See* Local area network
Land acquisition grant, x
Language
 economy of, 97
Laundering federal money, 137
Laurence, Helen, 109
Laws
 pertaining to contract project, 69
Layout
 in project narrative, 62
Least-served populations
 library services to, 27
Lefferts, Robert, 104
Letter of commitment
 to project, 137
Letter of inquiry, 137
Letter of intent, 45, 137
Letter of support, 138
Letter proposal, 45
Leveraging, 138
LEXIS/NEXIS (Mead-Data), 7
Librarians
 on grant development teams, 1, 125
Library media specialists
 role of, 69
Library Services Act (1965), 26
Library Services and Construction Act
  (LSCA), 26
 modified guidelines under, 27
Limitations statement
 to govern project, 34
Lin, Alvin C., 102
Linear regressions (simple)
 in inferential statistics, 84
Line-item budget, 71, 72, 75, 78
Listening, 20
Literacy programs, 27
Literacy Volunteers of Mid-Ohio Valley,
  116
Local area network (LAN), 151
Local needs assessments, 1
Local personnel, 66
Local programming plans
 reviewing, 43
Locke, Lawrence F., 104
Lump-sum budgets, 71, 72

Mainstreaming, 138
Major Urban Resource Libraries, 27
Mandate, 138
Maps
 in appendices, 60

Margins
 and proposal design, 61, 120
Matching, 138
Matching funds, 10, 77
 securing, 35
Matching funds budget
 sources of, 77
Matching grant, xi. *See also* Challenge
  grant
*Mathematics and Science Education
  Resources*
 web site, 105
Mathematics, Science, and Technology
  Education Programs That
  Work, 38
Maxwell, 7
Mbps (megabits per second), 151
McNeill, Patricia, 108
MCS. *See* Multiway Conferencing System
MCU (multipoint control unit), 151
Meador, Roy, 109
Means
 in descriptive statistics, 84
Mediaconferencing, 151
Membership fees
 for continuance funds, 58
Memorial gifts
 for continuance funds, 59
Mendell, Joy, 105
Mentor schools, 42
Mentors, 86
Merit raises, 126
Methodologies (project design), 35–37
Methods of payment, 90
Mhz (megahertz), 151
Mileage reimbursement rates, 75
Miller, Juliet V., 39
Missing components, 95, 96
Missing signatures, 95, 96
Mission statement, 6, 25
 in appendices, 59
 in file for proposal writing, 46
 importance of lucidity in, 26
 in introduction, 51
Modems, 143, 151
"Mother Targets Store for Grant," 114
MPEG (motion picture experts group),
  151
Multiplexer, 151
Multiplexing, 151
Multipocketed budgeting, 138
Multiway, 151
Multiway Conferencing System (MCS),
  152

Nakamura, Margaret, 114
Naming
    proposal, 49
Narrative, 138
National Endowment for the Humanities, 98
    web site, 106
National Guide to Funding for Libraries and Information Services, 104
"National Library Power Program," 111
National/Regional Resource Centers, 27
National Science Foundation
    web site, 106
Native-American groups
    library services to, 27
Needs assessment, 138
Needs statement, 49, 51–52, 124
    effective, 52
    in submission to funding source, 63
    unrealistic, 95
Negotiation process
    guidelines between funder and grant recipient, 89–90
    recommendations for, 79
Network, 152
Networking
    for locating evaluators, 85
New, Cheryl Carter, 109
News from ED
    web site, 112
Newsletters
    for dissemination, 57
    potential funder information in, 9
    publication of, 23
NIC (network interface card), 152
1996 Guide to Federal Funding for Education (Bernard, Feder, and Lin), 102, 109
Nondiscrimination, statement of, 64, 70
Nonpersonnel category
    and budget detail, 55
Nonprofit organizations, 98
    budgeting process for, 71
    and community foundations, 119
    grant issuers/grantees, 118
Norris, Dennis M., 109
Notification of Grant Award (NOGA)
    actions immediately following, 89
    activities for interim period prior to, 87–89
    communication channels surrounding, 88
NSCC Early Childhood Education (Drummond)
    web site, 111

NTSC (North American National Television System Committee), 152
Numeric databases
    access to, 7

Objectives
    and student learning, 36
    in submission to funding source, 63
Ogden, Thomas E., 109
Olson, David L., 109
111 Secrets to Smarter Grantsmanship, 109
Operating costs/expenses, 75
    sample budget, 76
    subdivisions of, 72
Operating foundations, 119
Operating grant, xi
Operations and maintenance costs, 121
Organization guidelines, 60–64
Organizational capability checklist, 35 (table 2-5)
Organizational commitment
    securing, 10
Organizational culture, 6
Organizational perspective
    applying, 20
Organizational qualifications
    establishing, 34
Orlich, Donald, 28, 31, 32, 34, 36, 110
Orlich, Patricia, 28, 31, 32, 34, 36
Outcome Funding: A New Approach to Targeted Grantmaking (Williams, Webb, and Phillips), 110
Outcome objectives, 53
Outlining process
    for proposal, 48
Out-of-band, 152
Overhead deficit, 138

Packaging, 139
Padded budgets
    and proposal failure, 95, 97
Page limits
    failure to comply with, 95, 96
PAL (phase alternate line), 152
Pamphlets
    for dissemination, 57
Pan/tilt camera, 152
Paper
    for project narrative, 62
Parents
    on grant development team, 1
    importance of collaboration with, 86
    involvement of, 98

Payout requirement, 139
Peer review, 139
Penn Library Grants and Research
   web site, 106
Per diem reimbursement rates, 75
"Percent of time," 74
Percentiles
   in descriptive statistics, 84
Performance (functional) budgets, 71, 72
Periodicals
   potential funder information in, 9
Personal interview schedules, 36
Personnel category
   and budget detail, 55
Personnel costs
   subdivisions of, 72
Personnel department
   and filling grant-funded positions, 91
Personnel expenses
   sample budget, 75
Personnel, key, 49
   in submission to funding source, 63
Philanthropists
   for continuance funds, 58
   disbursement of funds through, 98
Phillips, Virginia, 110
Phillips, William, 110
Physically handicapped persons
   library service for, 27
PI. *See* Principal investigator
Plan
   proposal function as, 48
Plan of action (project design), 53–54
Planning, ix, 1–24
   calendar development, 10–14
   decisions related to proposal prepara-
      tion, 18–24
   defined, 2
   historical commitment to, 5
   meetings for, 15–17
   pre-development process guidelines,
      9–10
   rationale for, 4
Planning grant, xi
Planning meetings
   conceptual design meeting, 17
   initial, 15, 17
Planning panel, 41
Point-to-multipoint, 152
Point-to-point, 152
Policy setting, 41
Political awareness, 21
Poor grantsmanship practices, 95–98
      (table 7-2)
POP (point of presence), 152

Postcards
   in submission to funding source, 63
Post-project development malaise, 87
"Power to Grow, The: Success Stories
      from the National Library Power
      Program" (Sadowski), 114
Pre-development planning
   guidelines for, 9–10
Preliminary reviewers, 139
Preliminary studies, 139
Pre-proposal, 139
Preservice development, 40
Press releases
   for dissemination, 57
PRI (primary rate interface), 150
Primary reviewer's report, 139
Principal investigator (PI), 129, 139
Print databases
   potential funder information in, 9
Printing, 72
Priorities
   setting, 13
Private funders
   and budget formatting, 77
Private grants, 117
   vs. government grants, 118
Pro bono publico, 140
Process objectives, 53
Professional development
   and grant development teams, 39
*Profiles of the Regional Educational
      Laboratories*, 38
Program budget, 71, 72, 73 (table 5-1).
      See also Budget; Budget
      development
Project
   conducting, 34
   defining, 33
Project accomplishments
   assessment of, 83
Project administration procedures
   timeline for, 91
Project advisory group
   establishment of, 41–42
Project calendar
   adjusting, 92
Project components and objectives
   identifying, 17 (table 1-6)
Project coordinator, 65
Project design, ix, 25–44, 49
   conceptual design, 33–37
   dynamic process underlying, 37–41
   mission statement, 26
   and parental involvement, 44
   project goal development, 26–30

and project management, 41–44
relationship between project goal statement and project objectives,
 30–32
in submission to funding source, 63
Project design (or plan of action), 53–54
Project design checklist, 33–34 (table 2-4)
Project director, 66–68
 activities during post-project development by, 88
 designating, 124
 formalizing hiring of staff by, 92
 post-award/funds receipt activities by,
  93
 responsibilities of, 67
Project documents
 for dissemination, 58
Project evaluation, ix, 81–86
 data collection methods, 83–84
 evaluation teams, 84–86
 methods, 82–83
 overview of evaluation process, 81
Project evaluators
 meetings with, 91
Project expenses
 division of, 72
Project goal development, 26–30
 in public libraries, 29–30
 in public school districts, 28–29
Project goal statement
 relationship between project objectives
  and, 30-32
 writing, 27
Project goals and objectives, 25
 and project narrative, 52–53
Project implementation, 90–92
Project management, 41–44
 project advisory group establishment,
  41–42
 in public libraries, 43–44
 for public school districts, 42–43
 training for advisory group members,
  42
Project management capability
 failure to describe, 95, 98
Project narrative, ix, 45–64
 and components of proposal, 49–60
 and cover letter, 60
 and proposal functions, 48
 proposal writing, design, and organization guidelines, 60–64
Project objectives
 guidelines development of, 31
 recommendations for, 30–31

relationship between project goal statement and, 30–32
Project personnel, ix, 65–70
 functional capabilities statements for,
  66–69
 local personnel available to project, 66
 provisions and assurances for, 69–70
 staffing requirements, 65–66
Project staff
 meetings with, 91
Project support, 40
Proofreading
 importance of, 97
 project narrative, 61
Proposal, 140
 activities following completion of, 87–98
 budget section of, 71
 components of, 49–60
 and cover letter, 60
 determining what funding agency is
  seeking, 120
 enlisting help in planning/writing, 124
 excerpts from, 56
 functions of, 48
 last-minute rushes in submitting, 125
 naming, 49
 organizing, 123
 resubmitting, 98
 specificity in, 121
 time allocation for writing of, 123
 typical length of, 121
Proposal budget preparation, 74 (table
  5-2)
Proposal development
 and parental involvement, 44
 problem analysis, 16 (table 1-5)
Proposal development calendar, 10–14,
  11–12 (table 1-3)
 modifying, 15
Proposal development specialist, 4
Proposal Development Tool Kit (New), 109
Proposal evaluator
 tips from, 120
Proposal preparation decisions
 document formatting issues, 19
 writing and editing issues, 18–19
Proposal scores
 obtaining, 88, 94
Proposal writers, 94
Proposal writing
 design and organization guidelines,
  60–64
 developing file in preparation for, 46–47
  (table 3-1)

Proposal writing (*continued*)
  managing, 13
  success and high standards in, 95
*Proposals That Work: A Guide for Planning
    Dissertations and Grant Proposals*
    (Locke, Spirduso, and Silverman),
    104
Provisions and assurances
  government compliances, 70
  hiring and employment compliances,
      69–70
Public libraries
  example project goals for, 29
  fund source assessment by, 15
  as grant seekers, ix
  professional development in, 40
  project goal development in, 29–30
Public library administrators/trustees, 43
Public school districts
  example project goals for, 29
  professional development in, 40
  project goal development in, 28–29
  specific information in proposal writing
      file for, 46–47
Public sector, 140
Publication grant, xi
Publications
  for continuance funds, 58
Punctuation
  errors in, 95, 97
Purchase requisitions
  writing, 91
Px64, 152
Pyramiding, 138

Qualifications
  determining, 74
  for project director, 68
  for project staff, 65–66
Qualitative data collection, 83, 84
Quantitative data collection, 83, 84
Questionnaires, 36
Quick, James A., 104, 109, 110

"Rakin' in the Clams . . . Or, How to Make
    Lots of Cash from Renting Best-
    Sellers" (Sumerford), 110
Rate-adapted videoconferencing, 152
Ratzlaff, Leslie, 110
Readability, 61, 120
Recordkeeping and management, 14
  on project transactions, 92

Reference documents
  maintenance of, 7
Reference tools
  for proposal development, 125
Regional consortiums
  and project support, 40
Reimbursement rates
  researching, 75
Renovation grant, xi
Reporting requirements, 17
Reports
  for dissemination, 58
  evaluation, 81
"Request the chair," 153
Requests for applications (RFAs), 1, 27,
    86, 88, 128, 140
  and project goal development, 26
Requests for proposals (RFPs), 27, 122,
    140
  analyzing, 1
  issuance of, 4
  and project goal development, 26
Requirements survey, 153
Research
  budget, 55
  design, 140
  for foundation grants, 119
  of potential funders, 1, 2, 95, 96
Research-based knowledge
  acquisition of, 39
Research findings
  for proposal development process, 7
Research grant, xi
Research implications
  and evaluation design, 49, 55–57
Research Proposals: A Guide to Success
    (Ogden and Goldberg), 109
Resolution, 153
*Resource Guide to Federal Funding for
    Technology in Education*
  web site, 106
Resources
  and organizational capability, 35
Retirees
  as evaluators, 85
Retirement funds, 75
Revenue sharing, 134, 140
Reviewers
  and abstracts, 50
Reviewer's comments
  obtaining, 88, 94
Reward system
  for staff contributions, 5–6
RFAs. *See* Requests for applications

RFPs. *See* Requests for proposals
RGB (red, green, blue), 153
Rife, Patricia, 114
"Right people"
  and obtaining grants, 120
Risk capital, 140
Risktaking, 7–8
Rockefeller Foundation, 119
Router, 153
RS-232, 153
RS-449, 153

Sacrifice trap, 140
Sadowski, Michael, 114
Salaries, 55, 72
  determining, 74
  and fringe benefits, 5
  and project director, 68
Salary continuation
  beyond funding period, 66
Sales piece
  proposal function as, 48
Sample of respondents, 36
Satellite, 153
Satellite uplink equipment, 153
School districts
  grants awarded to, 98
School media centers
  as grant seekers, ix
"School Media Matters: Grant World: It
  Pays to Play" (Kollasch), 109
School readiness
  improving, 43
School-to-Work Initiative, 117
Schumacher, Dorin, 104
Seed grant, xi, 141
Self-appraisal process, 94
Self-assessment tools
  organizational, 8–9 (table 1-2)
Self-instructional modules
  for dissemination, 58
Seminars, 39
  for dissemination, 57, 58
Sentence structure
  in project narrative, 61
Service delivery system, 141
Service fees
  for continuance funds, 58
Set-aside, 141
Shellow, Jill R., 105
Sign-off, 141
Silverman, Stephen J., 104
Single-subject design, 37
Site licensing, 153

Site visits, 39, 141
  for dissemination, 57
Skills assessment
  for grant development team, 17
Slow scan, 153
Social security contributions, 75
Soft match, 141
Soft money, 141
Software
  for document preparation, 19
  instructional and reference, 143
Solutions
  capacity of, 24
  identifying/evaluating, 22
  tasks for accomplishing of, 23
Southwest Educational Development
  Laboratory
  web site, 113
Southwestern Bell Science Education
  Center, The
  web site, 113
Space usage, 72
Spacing
  and proposal design, 61
Special project grant, xi
Specific objectives, 141. *See also* Behav-
  ioral objectives; Broad, long-term
  objectives
Spelling
  errors in, 95, 97
  in project narrative, 61
Spending
  plan for, 49
  plan for future, 58–59
Spinoff disease, 141
Spinoff projects, 141
Spirduso, Waneen Wyrick, 104
Sponsors, xi, 142
Staerkel, Kathleen, 110
Staff appearances
  for dissemination, 57
Staff contributions
  reward system for, 5
Staff development grants, 36
Staff development projects, 35
Staffing requirements
  and local personnel, 66
  for project, 65–66
State agencies
  and project support, 40
State board of control
  and reimbursement rates, 75
State funding
  decline in, 4, 126

State governments
  grants issued by, 118
State grant funding agencies
  hiring funds through, 66
Statement of nondiscrimination,
      64, 70
State of Texas
  web site, 113
Statistics
  in introduction, 51
  for quantitative data collection, 84
Stella, Nancy C., 105
Strategic plan
  and organizational capability, 35
*Strategies and Resources for Developing
      Quality Grant Applications*, 110
Student learning
  and project objectives, 36
Students
  on grant development team, 1
Subcontract, 79, 142
Subcontracting arrangements
  establishing, 91
Subcontractors, 70
Submission to funding source
  checklist of key components for, 63–64
      (table 3-2)
Subscription services
  potential funder information in, 9
Success
  factors working against, 95–98
  in obtaining grants, 123
Successful Proposal Writing Workshop,
      107
Sumerford, Steve, 110
Summative evaluation, 48, 55, 81, 83
Summative/product evaluation,
      142
Summative program evaluation, 2
Supplementary materials, ix
Supplies, 55, 70, 72
Support services, 142
Support staff
  on grant development team, 1
Survey instrument
  pretesting, 36
Surveys, 35
  vs. experimental studies, 36

Table of contents, 49, 50
  in submission to funding source, 63
Tables
  and project design, 54

Target population, 45, 142
  assessment of, 33
  and grant money spending, 121
  and introduction to proposal, 50, 51
Task completion dates, 17
Tasks
  efficacy of, 24
Tax Reform Act of 1969, 134
Taxes, 75
TDM. *See* Time division multiplexing
Tech Prep grants, 117
Technical assistance, 142
Technical review, 142
Technological developments
  and professional development, 40
Technology
  unjustified requests for, 95, 97
Technology and automation terms,
      143–155
Technology initiative activities, 41
Telecommuting, 154
Teleconferencing, 39, 154
Telethons
  for continuance funds, 59
10Base-T, 154
Tests
  in inferential statistics, 84
Texas Education Agency, 122
Thank-you letters, 90
Theoretical research, 142. *See also* Action
      research; Applied research
T-3 (DS-3), 154
Time commitments
  determining, 74
Time division multiplexing (TDM), 151
Time management. *See also* Project
      calendar
  and grantseeking, 13
Timelines, 54
  and award notification, 87
  for funder's cycle, 125
  for project administration procedures,
      91
Times New Roman font, 97
Timetables, 97
  drafting, 48
*Title I Today: A Comprehensive Overview
      of the Largest Federal Aid Program
      for Local Schools*, 110
Token ring, 154
T-1 (DS-1), 154
T-120, 154
Topic sentence, 142

Training
    employees, 70
    grant, xi
    opportunities, 5
Training sessions/workshops, 23, 58
Travel, 72
Twisted-pair cable, 154
Typefaces
    and proposal design, 61

Unemployment insurance, 75
Unexpended funds, 142
United Parcel Service
    pickup/delivery schedules for, 13
Unrestricted funds, 143
Unsolicited applications, 143
U.S. Department of Education
    web site, 106
*U.S. Department of Education Secretary's
    Initiatives*
    web site, 106
*U.S. Department of Education Technology
    Initiatives*
    web site, 107
*U.S. National Information Infrastructure
    Virtual Library*
    web site, 112
U.S. Philanthropy
    web site, 105
U.S. Postal Service
    pickup/delivery schedules for, 13
User charges
    for continuance funds, 58
UTP (unshielded twisted-pair wiring), 154

Validation projects, 35
Vanity funding 143. *See also*
    Begging/stealing
VCRs, 143
Vendor requisitions
    preparation of, 91
    submitting, 92
Verbose language, 95, 97
Video mixing, 155
Videoconferences, 39
Videophone, 155
Vienna (West Virginia) Public Library,
    116
Voice-activated multipoint videoconfer-
    encing, 155
Voice-only teleconferencing, 143
Volunteers, 24

Wages, 55
WAN. *See* Wide area network
Wave division multiplexing (WDM), 151
Webb, Arthur, 110
Welcome to the White House
    web site, 112
Welcome to WestEd
    web site, 113
Wesley United Methodist Church, 116
Whiteboard, 149
Wide area network (WAN), 155
Williams, Harold, 110
Winning Federal Grants: A Guide, 110
Winning Grant Proposals (Frost), 108
*Winning Grants Step by Step: Support
    Centers of America's Complete
    Workbook for Planning, Developing,
    and Writing Successful Proposals*
    (Carlson), 52, 103, 107
*Workforce Development Training
    Proposals*, 110
Working Group of advisory body, 42
Working papers
    for dissemination, 57
Workshops, 39
World Wide Web sites
    funding sources, 105–7
    project support tools, 110–12
    state and regional, 113
Writing, 1, 18–19. *See also* Proposal
    writing
    budget section of proposal, 55
    dull, 95, 96
    enlisting help in, 124
    grant proposal, 2
    project goal statement, 27
    project narrative, 60–62
    project objectives, 53
    purchase requisitions, 91
    time allocation for, 123
    and winning reviewer's attention, 50
Writing Grant Proposals That Win!, 108

Xerox, 148

Yahoo's List
    web site, 112
*Youth Services Librarians as Managers: A
    How-to Guide from Budgeting to
    Personnel* (Staerkel), 110

Zero-based budgets, 71, 72